MARGARET JONAS was the librarian at Rudolf Ste   rs, and has stu   er special in   n, astrology,   il, psychology   is-ness. She   *rit* and editor of an anthology by Rudolf Steiner on the subject. She has edited several other anthologies of Steiner's work and has written articles for various journals. She lives in Sussex, England, and has a son.

THE NORTHERN ENCHANTMENT

Norse Mythology, Earth Mysteries and Celtic Christianity

Margaret Jonas

TEMPLE LODGE

The Publishers would like to thank the Humanities Section of the School of Spiritual Science for its generous sponsorship of this publication

Temple Lodge Publishing
Hillside House, The Square
Forest Row, RH18 5ES

www.templelodge.com

Published by Temple Lodge 2013

A catalogue record for this book is available from the British Library

ISBN 978 1 906999 53 7

Cover by Andrew Morgan Design
Typeset by DP Photosetting, Neath, West Glamorgan
Printed and bound in the UK by 4edge Ltd, Essex

Contents

Introduction

For many people there is an enchantment and mystery associated with the concepts of 'north' or 'northern', which, leaving aside geographical locations in Britain, may be difficult to explain and may not appeal to everyone as they suggest the cold, the wintry, ice, fog and snow. But a few years ago a book appeared called *The Idea of North* by Peter Davidson, which set out to explore the fascination of 'north' felt by many writers, artists and explorers throughout various times and cultures.

> Everyone carries their own idea of north within them. The phrase 'true north' is itself a piece of geographer's precision, the difference between the northernmost point on the globe and the slight declination marked by the magnetic north to which the compass needle tends. The phrase has metaphoric force beyond the definition. 'True north' goes beyond the idea of the prodigious (or malign) north and suggests that, for each individual, there exists somewhere the place that is the absolute of the north, the north in essence, northness in concentration and purity.[1]

This book was in preparation a long time before *The Idea of North* was published, but reading it was a confirmation that for many there is indeed something magical associated with 'the north'. Davidson does not explore the spiritual side of the attraction, which this book seeks to do. It is an attempt to show how, through ancient history, Norse-Germanic mythology and more recent studies of carefully aligned sacred sites, a truer Christianity found expression in the British Isles, Ireland, Scandinavia and Germany (northern Russia, Siberia or Alaska are beyond its scope). Ancient beliefs about divine beings connected with the sun were fulfilled through the coming of Christ, and a new spiritual wisdom gradually spread across Europe, not only from the south northwards (as generally assumed) but from west to east, as once there had been voyagers travelling from east to west.

We are attempting to show that a paradisaical essence from the earliest stages of earth evolution was not entirely lost but continued to live on as if preserved in hidden places as a source of inspiration and that these places, whether or not they had an actual geographic location or whether they dwelt somewhere within the human soul, were associated with the idea of 'the north.'

Norse-Germanic mythology, Rudolf Steiner pointed out, offers the best basis for our age in understanding anthroposophy. We are not attempting to discuss the whole of it, only certain pertinent features. One aspect is, however, worth mentioning here as it has become a matter of contemporary concern. The myths tell us that the first man and woman were created from two trees; they were called Ask and Embla. Ask is the ash and Embla is generally assumed to mean the elm. Readers will hardly need reminding that both these particular trees are under attack—the elm from Dutch elm disease since roughly the 1930s and, much more recently, 'ash dieback' (*Chalara fraxinea*), now spreading across Europe and threatening the ash. It is said to be the ash, moreover, that is *Yggdrasil*, the Tree of Life. This has led some commentators to suggest that because the burning of Yggdrasil was the beginning of Ragnarok, the 'Twilight of the Gods', an apocalyptic Ragnarok is now beginning. This is not an attempt to minimize the seriousness of 'ash dieback' and the threat to a much loved and familiar tree, but Ragnarok, according to Steiner, began much further back. It was the loss of the old clairvoyance, the ability of human beings to see into the spiritual world and communicate with its gods. They 'withdrew' and humanity was left to develop independence. The myths foretell a promise of new life after Ragnarok, which as we shall show has already begun.

It seems to me that although the dangers to the environment cannot be overlooked and must be addressed urgently, the *real* threat is to the human being—Ask and Embla. It is the human being who is the real battleground for the adversary powers and no one, from little children to the elderly, is safe from their attacks which take many forms—often disguised as 'beneficial' or 'necessary' in some way. It is the free thinking potential of the human being hindered by doubt so that everything becomes relative and is only a matter of 'opinion'; the soul and heart which are the basis for our moral truthfulness, our 'human' values, and are instead led into lies and mockery; and the will or deeds which are constantly being hindered and paralysed by fear in all forms. This book does not claim to have answers but offers the possibility, as we consider the more hidden aspects of history, of our being able to find strength for reaching our future goals.

*   *   *

In E.M. Forster's novel *Howards End*, the character Margaret Schlegel says that the English have no mythology. I contest that she is incorrect. It is there—it has only to be recognized.

*   *   *

In the interests of clarity I have used the simplified, more common English versions of Norse-Germanic names (there are various versions anyway within this language family). Sadly English no longer includes the letters ð and þ (still found in Icelandic) for the two 'th' sounds, so we must make do with 'd 'and 'th' and hope the reader may bear this in mind when coming to the quotations from the Edda.

1. The Early Northern Mysteries

Ah! What came we forth to see that our hearts are so hot with
   desire?
Is it enough for our rest, the sight of this desolate strand,
And the mountain-waste voiceless as death but for the winds
   that may sleep not nor tire?
Why do we long to wend forth through the length and breadth
   of a land,
Dreadful with grinding ice, and record of scarce hidden fire,
But that there 'mid the grey grassy dales sore scarred by the
   ruining streams
Lives the tale of the Northland of old and the undying glory of
   dreams?

William Morris[2]

'From Greenland's icy mountains . . .' What images are evoked by a
northern landscape—a vast region of cold snowy wastes over-
shadowed by silent pine forests, shimmering lakes reflecting bril-
liant starlight, the northern lights, the midnight sun? Is it a search
for an outer purity to match an inner longing? Clear air, unsullied
whiteness, landscapes unspoiled by human greed. Some ancient
chord is echoed when we hear of the land 'at the back of the north
wind' or 'land of the midnight sun' as though it bears a beauty too
terrible to look upon. Winters without day and summers without
night—nature's rhythms are mysterious and must play upon the
psyche. In long fearful winters we can imagine the frost giants still
casting the land into a freezing, crystalline world. Who dares to
travel to the Snow Queen's palace without risk of an ice splinter
lodging in the heart? Then there are the white nights where a low-
hung sun suggests everlasting summers and lands of youth and joy.
To the Greeks these regions were as wondrous as was Tír-nan-Óg to
the Celts—the land of the ever-young. *Hyperborea*—beyond the
north wind (Boreas), *Ultima Thule*—these are some journeys we
shall be taking.

   In spiritual science Hyperborea has a special meaning. It is the
name of an earlier stage of the earth's evolution when it was very

young indeed, far earlier than sunken legendary Atlantis.[3] During this epoch human beings were not at all as they are today. They were androgynous, plantlike, having bodies of etherlife force rather than of physical matter. The earth was remembering the even earlier stage of evolution when all was Sun and the future ether forces for all creation were formed by the sacrifice of spiritual beings, the Kyriotetes or Spirits of Wisdom. This was when the etheric or life forces were first bestowed on the hitherto cosmic organism of 'warmth'. In the later, Hyperborean period, the sun separated from the earth to form a rhythmically spiralling and rotating etheric body of sun and earth with the future planets Mercury and Venus in between. Spiritual beings connected with the sun withdrew with it, in the service of the great Sun Spirit who was to be recognized under many names: Ahura Mazda, Lugh, Baldur, Christ.

In order to understand the ideas put forward here, we shall begin by trying to gain a better grasp of the 'etheric', which is not the same as the 'ether' proposed by nineteenth-century scientists. The following cannot really be explained so simply and thus studying the relevant literature is suggested. But when we speak about the etheric or field of life forces we learn how there are four kinds of 'ether', which correspond to the four elements: warmth ether (fire), light ether (light/air), sound, chemical, tone ether (water), life ether (earth). The last two may be less obvious. The chemical or tone ether is so-called because it has formative properties in that the building blocks of substances are brought together by a force of attraction. Chemical elements are combined due to the action of this ether. That this formative quality is connected to tone or sound can be demonstrated by the Chladni equipment—a fine powder placed on a plate and then struck with a tuning fork will form harmonious patterns. More elaborate experiments with acoustical equipment have been devised, and the work of Masaru Emoto regarding water's crystalline patterns is becoming better known.[4] The life ether is perhaps more elusive as it is living force in matter. Whether or not the 'third force' Steiner mentioned as its counterpart is the same as atomic power is too complex to debate here, but radio-activity is said to be a result of 'decaying' life ether. It is possible that Wilhelm's Reich's experiments in America in the 1950s to harness 'orgone energy' was a manifestation of life ether, as this apparently had the power to counteract radioactivity. Aubrey Westlake sums up Reich's experiments thus:

> Phase One. Nuclear energy affects orgone energy in a most damaging manner.
> Phase Two. Orgone energy after the first blow fights back ferociously. It runs mad, runs beserk—this is DOR [deadly orgone energy] producing radiation sickness.
> Phase Three. If orgone energy has the opportunity to keep fighting nuclear energy it will finally succeed in rendering nuclear energy harmless. It will replace the noxious secondary activity of the nuclear energy by penetration of the nuclear energy matter, and will put it at its service.[5]

Reich was imprisoned and his research materials seized for his attempt to harness life ether with the intention of helping humanity.

Steiner also revealed that electricity is 'fallen' or 'decayed' light ether—or 'light mastered by gravity'[6]—and magnetism 'fallen' chemical/sound ether. And with the phenomena of the auroras we may see the earth's magnetism and electricity already returning to an etheric condition—as if something is being prepared in advance for the future transformation of the earth.

When the sun withdrew it left behind a concentration of etheric forces in the polar regions. Hans Mändl has pointed out that the earth has a 'breathing' rhythm in this connection.[7] At the poles there remains an ether concentration which does not sink so deeply into the earth. In a 24-hour period, the earth's breathing rhythm has its maximum 'breathing out' eastwards at around 3 p.m. (3 a.m. in the southern hemisphere), then its deepest 'breathing in' westwards at 3 a.m. (or 3 p.m. for the antipodes)—a continuous process of maximum and minimum at 3 p.m. and 3 a.m. It is interesting to note in connection with this that the maximum and minimum of liver activity in the human body also occur at 3 p.m. and 3 a.m. The liver, as its name reveals, is the organ particularly related to the etheric—*life* forces. These rhythms of breathing and their connection with the differentiated ethers are shown more fully in Guenther Wachsmuth's pioneer work *The Etheric Formative Forces in Cosmos, Earth and Man*.[8]

Due to later shifts of the earth's axis the poles are now tilted at an angle of 23 ½° towards the sun in summer and away from it in winter, which accounts for the fact of freezing polar winters and lack of daylight. The magnetic poles are where the concentrated regions of life ether show a heightened activity (see Wachsmuth for a much fuller account). The earth's electricity is also released more strongly here as the sun, which destroys it, is weakest. Instead the moon forces are strong and contribute to the phenomena of the aurora borealis, or northern (and southern) lights, with their magical displays of shimmering colour.[9] Goethe's colour experiments show that for colour to arise light must meet with darkness or matter.[10] The earth's electricity is 'fallen' light ether and when this meets with the matter-potential forces of the chemical and life ethers, which are so intense at the poles, the colours can appear.

The 'polar' region referred to by Mändl is also much larger than the extreme points of the geographic poles. He suggests it starts from latitude 60° north and south—the point at which countries in these latitudes such as Scandinavia and northern Russia enjoy their 'white nights' of summer and long dark winters. Because of the tilt of the earth's axis in relation to the cosmos, the sun and certain zodiacal constellations do not properly rise or set during winter. For an astrologer this means that a horoscope cannot be cast in the usual way as there is no daily 'rising sign', the Ascendant, or culmination (the Midheaven). The effect of this on a not inconsiderable proportion of the earth's population, when we take northern Scandinavia, Siberia, northern Canada and northern Mongolia into account, has not yet been researched it would seem. This is something of a digression, but it is meant to show how the human being's life and breathing processes are intimately bound up with the earth's. The experiences of summer and winter are further accompanied by an expansion or contraction of the soul life. In the Hibernian mysteries of the west, the neophyte was led to a strong inner experience of summer and winter landscapes.[11] What was taught there could be experienced strongly as nature processes in the far north, which is perhaps why Richard Seddon suggests pupils in the Arthurian mysteries (which were guided from the Hibernian centres) were sent to northern mystery centres also.[12]

Because of earlier people's awareness of the earth's rhythms and the concentration of ether forces at the pole, far back in these times the northern regions were thought to be a land of everlasting life or renewal of life where special beings might be found. For in the very ancient epoch of the earth after the Hyperborean known as the 'Lemurian', before Atlantis, there were apparently beings who dwelt in the polar region who had poorly developed physical bodies but highly developed ether bodies with great clairvoyant faculties. They could understand the wisdom of the stars and the hierarchies of spiritual beings; they belonged to a group soul of an advanced nature. They can be thought of as living in the air in a kind of paradise and were not properly dependent on the earth. They were to develop in time into the more advanced human beings of Atlantis.

> So we can say that the North Pole was populated by people that actually lived in the realms of air in a kind of paradise, and who had not yet descended as far as the earth ... you can now compare with what you encounter here and there in anthroposophical literature, namely that those higher beings who were once the teachers of mankind descended from the cold North! We have actually found them, the group souls around the North Pole.[13]

We have to remember that *physical* conditions at the poles were likely to have been very different so far back. Elsewhere, Steiner refers to these beings as 'Sun-men' or 'Apollo-men'.[14] The idea that there was a northern paradise-like region on earth called Hyperborea or Thule has thus come down through the mythology of both Greek and northern peoples.

Aeons later than the period of Hyperborea in the continent of Atlantis before it sank beneath the waves of the Atlantic Ocean, which is named after it, knowledge of the secrets of the etheric had been kept alive in the Sun mystery centres. From these, people who had not dabbled in the black magic which brought about the destruction of Atlantis were chosen to migrate to the land masses of northern Europe and Asia. The more northerly stream of people retained a closer connection with the Sun-ether mysteries, and amongst these were the more closely guarded secrets which were held in centres in the north of what is now Scandinavia and Russia. These were the centres of the Drotts or Trotten, closely related to those of the earliest so-called 'Druids'.[15]

The leader of the northern stream was an initiate, Skythianos. At this time he remained with those who settled in the European regions but was later to incarnate in the region of the Black Sea and guide the peoples known as Scythians. His fellow initiate was to have many incarnations as Zarathustra, and he led his followers further into Asia. Because of this the later mythologies of the Germanic and Iranian peoples were to show a close connection. In Ireland, Skythianos laid the seeds of the Hibernian mysteries of the west.[16] His special mystery knowledge was of the nature of the physical body, of matter, and how ego-consciousness could be developed in it. This was to develop in the later northern mysteries and we shall see how it is specially revealed as the earthly counterpart of 'Asgard'.

At this point we should make a distinction between streams. Steiner refers to a northern mystery stream contrasted with a southern. The former comprises all of Europe, including the so-called Apollonian Greek mysteries, Russia and Iran. The mysteries involved a penetration of outer nature forces and beings, and was a more macrocosmically inclined culture. The southern stream mysteries depended on a penetration of the human soul life and the inner bodily organs. It was found in ancient Egypt, Babylon and Chaldea and the 'Dionysian' Greek mysteries. Thus there was both an outer and an inner Threshold crossing.[17] The southern 'inner' one was considered more dangerous than the 'outer' northern one and the mysteries were more carefully guarded. Within the broader northern stream (which includes the western) there is also a more specific northern stream of which we are speaking here, encompassing the geographical regions that will be discussed.

People in the later Atlantean periods possessed a kind of light within them which could illuminate the night, an astral consciousness, a kind of inner 'midnight sun' and the purpose of the mystery schools was partly to recover this ancient state.[18] All initiations result in a loosening of the etheric and astral bodies from the physical. In the northern regions the schooling was by penetrating into outer nature through the senses, allowing the etheric body to be loosened in a state of ecstasy, the astral body and ego (as far as it was developed then) to be lifted out, making way for a higher consciousness to fill the human being. This means of initiation is still a feature of shamanic practices today.

The early priest-initiates of the north were called the Trotten or Drotts, or Druids—as they came to be known in western countries. The methods taught by the Trotten required twelve initiate helpers who surrounded the thirteenth. Each had developed a different characteristic or skill so that the twelve were a reflection of the twelve signs of the zodiac.[19] King Arthur's round table with twelve principal knights was a later western development of this spiritual archetype. The Trotten or Trott mysteries extended as far as northern Russia. Sergei Prokofieff refers to the stone carvings and 'sun labyrinths' of stones that can be seen scattered throughout the western shores of the White Sea down to Lake Onega.[20] The original leader in the north was Sieg or Sigge, who gave his name to the later legendary hero Sigurd or Siegfried. Sigurd has to overcome his lower nature—the dragon. He was filled with the spiritual being of Odin/Wotan/Woden.[21] Odin or Wotan, whom Steiner has revealed as really being an archangel, was known as a god as far back as the Atlantean peoples, although the mythology about him did not develop until approximately the beginning of the fourth post-Atlantean epoch (*c.* 747 BC).[22]

In 1904 Rudolf Steiner expressed the connection between Odin and Sieg like this:

> Everywhere in these northern regions the Druid [*sic*] initiation was still practised ... one can say its chief founder was named Sieg ... Odin is the highest initiate of the northern mysteries ... Sieg was therefore the Chela [occult pupil] of the north who placed his body at the disposal of the higher, more spiritual Odin.[23]

And later in 1908:

> It was felt that the gods had to withdraw from the world they had themselves created. The gods who, even as late as the Atlantean epoch, had descended into the bodies of the most advanced human beings and had taught them important secrets in the Mysteries were obliged gradually to withdraw, and they could only come in touch with the physical world by using the more advanced human beings as their instruments or vehicles ... those who were initiated into the ancient Druidic

Mysteries knew, for example, that an ancient Atlantean individuality known as Sig [*sic*] appeared for long after the Atlantean catastrophe in many different ways in European bodies. All such names as Siegfried and Sigurd preserve exoterically the remembrance of the repeated appearances of this individuality who was finally only perceptible to those who had been initiated into the Mysteries.[24]

In the mystery centres the neophyte had to experience the 'death of Baldur', the loss of the light—the disappearing ancient clairvoyance. And through various trials and ordeals Baldur must be sought again.[25] In the myths, the slaying of Baldur brought about the Twilight of the Gods—Ragnarok (Götterdämmerung). The feeling that the gods were losing their connection with the earth they had created gave rise to this soul state. The story is that Baldur the sun god was so beautiful that his mother Frigga got every living creature and every plant to promise not to harm him. The gods delighted in the sport of throwing all sorts of missiles at him as they would not hurt him. But she did not take the promise from the mistletoe because it looked so young and innocent. The jealous adversary god Loki therefore made arrow shafts of mistletoe and persuaded Baldur's blind brother Hodur to hurl them at him. Baldur was killed—he could have been rescued from the underworld kingdom of Hel because all the world wept for him—had they indeed all wept for him. But one did not weep—Loki in disguise—and so Hel would not release him. It is possible that the old song *Who killed Cock Robin* is a much later echo of this myth.

The Druids

There is a problem of discrepancy between Steiner's term 'Druid' as synonymous with the earliest northern initiates and the term as understood more generally as being the priests of the Celtic peoples who spread westwards from central and eastern Europe much later. It seems likely that the Celtic tribes inherited and carried on the tradition of having Druid priests. When they migrated westwards from central Europe to the regions most associated with them—Britain, Ireland, France—they would have found and recognized 'Druids' or Drotts existing from earlier times, though recently there have been doubts raised as to the number of so-called Celts who actually emigrated from mainland Europe and whether indeed they were later 'pushed back westwards' by Anglo-Saxon conquerors as was previously supposed. Studies of blood types and DNA have revealed a more homogenous peoples existing in the British Isles from very early times, though their customs and language altered.[26] That a Germanic language predominated over Celtic languages except in the far west is certainly the case, but physical conquest is not necessarily the reason. In fact Jürgen Spanuth states that 'the ancient authors could not distinguish between the Celts and the Germans. Orosius (fifth century AD) described the Germans as one of the Celtic tribes. Livy (59 BC–AD 17) also described the Cimbri, Teutons and Ambrones as Celts.' Spanuth goes on to show that there are many more theories about a megalithic culture reaching across the whole of Europe from the far north and west to the Mediterranean than is commonly supposed.[27] Steiner's view is of a very early fairly homogenous northern and western spiritual culture which evolved throughout this north-west part of Europe. This culture was responsible for erecting the astronomically aligned stone circles and other megaliths still to be found in the British Isles and Ireland and a few other more western sites. It may be that Steiner refers more to secluded small groups of initiates rather than to the general mass of the peoples. What was practised in seclusion in mystery centres by a few would much later be more widely disseminated. By the time we hear of the Druids from legends, sagas and from Caesar's *Gallic Wars* a later stage has been reached and they are the recognized priests. Earlier, the Drotts or 'Druids' or in the far west, the Hibernian initiates developed their own spiritual knowledge more secretly. They organized or allowed what was appropriate for the age to be carried out in ritual and religious-cultic practice. There were many sacred cultic sites but only a few actual mystery centres.

According to Dudley Wright's *Druidism*, the first priests in Britain were called *Truti*—a word related to *Trotten*.[28] Much later, the Saxons called a sorcerer *dry*—related to Druid. One source of these words is said to be the word for *oak*. Groves of oak trees were sacred places to the northern peoples; in a much more thickly forested Europe one can easily imagine that such secluded centres existed. The stone circles were by contrast built on open heath and moorland because the stars and sun shadows must be visible for their purposes.

> The people of the New Stone Age and particularly their priests, the Druids, closely watched the changes that occurred in the natural world through the seasons and studied the ways in which these rhythmical changes depended on the powers of the sun and the moon. They built instruments of stone (dolmen, stone circles) that permitted them to 'see through' the way in which the powers of sun and moon combined in the different seasons. They took an interest in everything that was alive and active and thus revealed to them the will of the gods.[29]

> Because of the initiation he had received, the Druid priest was able to see right through the Druid stones. He saw the currents flowing downwards, not the physical sunlight that had been blocked off, but the spiritual and soul qualities that live in the physical sunlight. This inspired him with all that flowed into his wisdom about the spiritual cosmos, the great universe. At other times of day the opposite happened; currents flowed up from the earth. These could be observed when the sun was not shining on the place. In these upward currents lived the moral qualities of the congregation for which the priest was responsible, so that at certain times the priest was able to see the moral qualities of the congregation that surrounded him.[30]

Rudolf Steiner's 'Druid Stone' sketch, inspired by his visits to Ilkley and Penmaenmawr in 1923, suggests heavenly wisdom and knowledge of the creative forces being brought down by higher priests to another level below and finally to the ordinary folk.

Whether or not a hierarchy is implied, there are three levels in the sketch. At Ilkley there is such a possibility in the physical landscape: a stone circle high on Rombald's moor, then lower down but above the town on an outcrop of rock the engraving of a swastika or fylfot, in this case representing the 'four-petalled lotus flower' or base chakra.

> Quite near Ilkley there is a hill like this, with a stone at the top marked with what is essentially a swastika—although it is a

The Druid Stone, *a sketch by Rudolf Steiner*

little more complicated. Such signs were carved into stones sited in specific places. They indicate a spot where the Druid priest was filled with the ideas that were culturally creative about two or three thousand years ago in these parts... What can you read in these signs as you stand before a stone of this kind? You read the words that lived in the Druid priest's heart: 'Behold, the eye of the senses sees the hills and the places where human beings dwell. The eye of the spirit, the lotus flower, the spinning lotus flower (for the swastika is a sign of this) sees into human hearts and looks into the inmost parts of the soul. Through my seeing I desire to be united with those who have been entrusted to me as my congregation.'[31]

The Druids underwent an initiation into the forces of the sun. They recognized the spiritual being of the Sun God, and that the sun was then the outer garment or dwelling place for him. They learnt to read the constellations of the zodiac as if they were a heavenly script and came to know the different forces of Aries or Taurus, etc. which were revealed to clairvoyant sight by contemplating the shadows thrown by megaliths. They could thus teach the people when sowing must take place or when the bull must impregnate the cows. Their knowledge was thus brought into practical use. They could also perceive the work of elemental beings, the nature spirits in the growth of plants and in the wind, rain, frost and snow—we might still speak about 'Jack Frost' to children. They understood how

The swastika stone, Ilkley Moor, Yorkshire

earlier forces from the time when the moon was still part of the earth worked on within the earth in the form of currents known as serpent or dragon energy, and practised the appropriate 'serpent magic' to harness and contain these. They would have known which parts of the earth had special life forces and how to lay out sacred sites to enhance these. This mystery knowledge continued right down into the Middle Ages when churches were built with understanding for the etheric nature of a site. There are many legends throughout Europe of church building being interfered with by supernatural or animal means—stones are mysteriously taken down by night and frequently an animal leads people to the correct site. Certain aspects of this knowledge will be discussed further in Chapter 6.

Earth currents play into health and illness and are particularly related to the forces of the human will, especially in connection with metabolism and digestion, the breaking down of foodstuffs and physical reproduction. An understanding of the harmful effects of currents with which the human 'double' becomes connected and how these are stronger in some regions than in others was described by Rudolf Steiner in lectures given in St Gallen on 'Geographic Medicine'.[32] This 'double' is intimately bound up with the electro-magnetic forces of the earth and is of an 'ahrimanic' nature, affecting the etheric body. Human beings also have a 'double' connected more with their soul life—the 'luciferic' double—but the two inevitably interweave and affect each other. The 'geographic' effect was a mystery knowledge probably known in later Atlantis because the oldest Atlantean streams, namely the Chinese and the Native Americans, had a knowledge of it. Both for instance revered the Great Spirit, the Tao or Taotl. The Chinese still have these traditions—'feng shui', an understanding of the dragon energy in the earth and in the human body and especially how any buildings need to be harmonized by taking note of this in order for the occupants to be healthy (though it has to be said that nowadays this has degenerated somewhat into more superstitious beliefs concerning wealth and success). The Native Americans likewise have a tradition of understanding the sacredness of the earth—which places, rocks or plants have a special quality, which creatures will help them in their 'medicine', which is their mystery knowledge.

Before and right into the early centuries after Christ, Norse and

Irish peoples sailed to America to study the forms of illness in people and how the earth currents affected them there. The *Vinland Sagas*[33] describe such voyages, though written down later, also the 'Zeno narrative' and the voyage of Prince Henry Sinclair,[34] though no mention is made of the secrets of illness and healing. Archaeological digs have revealed artefacts from Europe of this period, especially in Newfoundland, and the fact of the Norsemen being the first travellers to America is now more widely accepted. The voyages were stopped for a time, perhaps not more than a period of 100 years, by edict of the Pope in order to protect Europeans from what was thought to be inimical—and Columbus was then allowed to 'discover' America. Why was there so much obfuscation and doubt thrown on the records of earlier navigators? Papal documents have come to light which reveal knowledge of these ancient routes, but because of the suppression just referred to, Columbus having visited Iceland was doubted because he was not 'supposed to have known' about these old sea routes.[35]

The unusual physical nature of volcanic Iceland was part of this mystery knowledge, and Greenland, which was truly 'green' and milder in the early Middle Ages, allowed for Norse settlements for several centuries. The climate change that resulted in Greenland's becoming much colder and barren contributed to the mythology of Thule—was it Iceland or was it part of Norway? We will look at the possibilities later. Even modern Icelandic stories such as the crime fiction of Arnaldur Indriason describe a landscape which is alive in a way that is often hauntingly menacing.

Ireland is a region where these ancient moon currents were least present in their harmful form. Because of this the legend arose that St Patrick had driven out all the snakes from Ireland, and none are to be found there now unless imported. The clairvoyant power of the Druids was particularly unimpaired here so that they were even able to perceive the death of Christ as it occurred. This is shown in the legend of King Conchubar who had in the top of his head a ball made from the brains of his enemy. One Friday he noticed unusual changes in the sky and his chief Druid was wailing and grieving, so the king asked what ailed him. The Druid replied that in a far away land the people had killed the Sun God. King Conchubar was so angry at what these people had done that he began slashing at the trees with his sword, imagining himself to be avenging the Sun God's death. As a result the ball burst from his brain and he died.[36]

In Britain and northern Europe awareness of the dragon-serpent energies in the earth was handed down through the centuries. To protect people the Archangel Michael, most famous of dragon-slayers, has hilltops and many churches dedicated to him. In their book *The Sun and the Serpent* the authors Hamish Miller and Paul Broadhurst[37] have a traced a 'Michael' line connecting many of these sites right across Britain, from Cornwall's western tip to East Anglia. In Norse-Germanic mythology we find the long saga of Sigurd or Siegfried the dragon-slayer. When Sigurd roasted the dragon Fafnir's heart and tasted its blood, he could 'understand the speech of the birds'—he had become an initiate. The story of Sigurd is to be found engraved on stone crosses in northern Britain, such as at Halton in Lancashire and on the Isle of Man—sites of Viking settlements as well as in Scandinavia—a reminder that Norse myths belong to the British Isles also. Several of the Norwegian stave churches, such as Borgund or Hopperstad, display dragons' heads on the roofs flying forth like the old Viking ships' prows. And indeed it has been pointed out how the churches are shaped like upturned Viking ships, and some had images of Sigurd carved round the doorways such as at Hylestad (a now demolished church but the panels can be seen in Oslo). The Old English poem *Beowulf* describes Beowulf's fight against a dragon-like monster, Grendel, and a further legend told, by Geoffrey of Monmouth, how King Vortigern of the Britons was unable to build a tower until Merlin had the ground drained, whereupon a red and a white dragon were revealed asleep in the swamp (suggesting etheric-electrical polarity?).[38] England's patron saint St George has a red and white cross as his emblem though he apparently hails from further south—it was the returning Crusaders who brought knowledge of him to England where Edward III may have been the first to name him as patron saint in 1348,[39] an echo perhaps of the red on white cross of the Templars. In Celtic Christian prayers St Michael is sometimes called the 'red-white'. And finally St Margaret was remembered as another dragon-slayer, especially in Norse-influenced Scotland.

2. Hyperborea, Thule and Apollo

Before discussing Hyperborea, we must first look at certain issues concerning the other principal name for this mythical region: Ultima Thule, an island, land mass or region often identified with Hyperborea. Pytheas of Massilia (Marseille), 340–285 BC, sailed across the seas for six days beyond Scotland. From north Shetland he may have gone to Iceland or to Norway, but he claimed to have reached 'Thule' and, one day north of it, a frozen sea. The difficulty now is not establishing where Thule actually was but of facing up to the myths of Thule and why they aroused the interest of the Nazi party. The Thule Gesellschaft was founded in 1918 by Rudolf von Sebottendorf as a Bavarian branch of the Germanenorden, which had strongly racist aims and so-called 'ideals' in which Thule was imagined as a mythical 'Aryan' homeland.[40] Other somewhat right-wing authors such as Julius Evola have shared these interests and there were Nazis who also hoped to discover the Grail. This should not mean that myths about Thule nor indeed Norse-Germanic mythology generally should be discredited because the Nazis misused aspects of it for their own terrible ends. Wagner's appropriation and somewhat distortion of the myths has not helped either. The swastika is an ancient spiritual symbol and the rune ⚡ is not inherently evil. But because of the horrible ends to which these ideas about Thule and the Germanic peoples ultimately led, it is enough for some people to feel that the whole subject is tainted and that interest in it may be somewhat suspect. Figures like Evola, more-over, have developed a personal 'masculine northern solar' cult as opposed to a 'feminine southern' one. This kind of polarization is a further highly undesirable development, but because these myths have been abused, however evilly, does not discredit their original worth and truth. The Nazis' misuse of the swastika emblem, which is engraved on the rocks above Ilkley, is sometimes said to be a 'demonic' use of an ancient sun symbol as it was 'reversed'. In fact swastikas have appeared turning both clockwise and anticlockwise for far longer and there is no evidence that 'reversal' has an evil intent. The constellation of the Great Bear or Odin's Wagon (as it was known in the north) appears to 'turn' about the Pole Star as it is

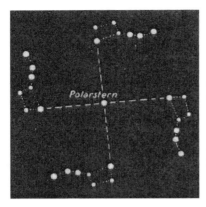

The Great Bear *constellation appears to change position in relation to the Pole Star in the European midnight sky. The positions when observed at the beginning of March, June, September and December create a swastika form. (Diagram from Ortrud Stumpfe,* Absturz in den Selbstverrat. Rhythmik in der germanischen Mythologie und der deutsch-europäische Geschichte, *Mellinger Verlag 1993.)*

revealed in the European midnight sky at the beginning of March, June, September and December, and thus forms a swastika pattern during the course of a year.[41]

Northern peoples imagined the turning of the heavens as the turning of a giant mill. Steiner described the emblem at Ilkley as being the 'four-petalled lotus flower' or base chakra rather than a sun symbol. The principal Nazi 'philosophy' or motive was racial—the obsessive idea of supposedly 'pure' or 'impure' races. It is through the base chakra that we are connected to our racial heritage and family. For the ancient peoples of Ilkley it may simply have been a tribal marking as was appropriate for those times, but for the Nazis we suggest that 'race' was the main reason for the use of this occult emblem.

Rudolf Steiner set out the value of the Norse-Germanic mythology as follows:

> We have no wish to introduce Orientalism and Occidentalism into what we look upon as the life-blood of Spiritual Science; if we should discover in the realm of the Nordic and Germanic Archangels a source of potential nourishment for true Spiritual Science, then this will not be the prerogative of a particular people or tribe in the Germanic countries, but of the whole of humanity. What is given to all mankind must be given; it may, it is true, originate in a particular region, but it must be given to the whole of humanity.[42]

It is precisely the future-orientated, universal potential of Germanic mythology that was seized by the Nazis and distorted for their own ends, part of which was to crush those spiritual movements such as anthroposophy, which teaches of the true nature of the Christ and of the free development of all human egos. For some people myths of Hyperborea and the northern lands will always be unappealing and, after two World Wars with Germany, almost unknown. But the spiritual basis inspired many writers in the nineteenth century, such as William Morris, and in the twentieth century W.H. Auden, C.S. Lewis, J.R. Tolkien and, more recently, novelists A.S. Byatt and Philip Pullman. It is the mythology of part of our own heritage in Britain—and of many English-speaking people worldwide. We deny part of our own make-up if we choose to ignore or devalue it.

* * *

We cannot understand the mythology of Hyperborea without referring to the beliefs of the ancient Greeks concerning their sun god, Apollo. Although associated mostly with Delos and Delphi his cult was also significant in Thrace and the Balkans; for instance, statues of Apollo in his swan-drawn chariot have been found in graves in the former Yugoslavia. We will consider later how Thrace was possibly the home of the common origin of the Greek and runic alphabets. Apollo is connected with both Greece and northern Europe and has a counterpart as we shall see in the Norse god Freyr— Apollo and his twin sister Artemis correspond in a certain sense (but are not identical with) Freyr and his sister Freya.

For three (or sometimes six) months of the year Apollo was said to fly north in his swan-drawn chariot to the blessed land of the Hyperboreans where there was neither disease nor old age, but bliss and eternal spring. We may recall that Steiner referred to the earliest human ancestors in Hyperborea as Sun-men or Apollo-men. The poet Alcaeus wrote in about 600 BC:

> O King Apollo, son of great Zeus, whom thy father did furnish forth at thy birth with golden headband and lyre of shell, and giving thee moreover a swan-drawn chariot to drive, would have thee go to Delphi ... But nevertheless, once mounted, thou badest thy swans fly to the land of the Hyperboreans.[43]

The poet Pindar (*c.* 522–443 BC) went on to write:

> But neither by sea nor by travelling by land canst thou dis-
> cover the wondrous path to the assembly of the Hyper-
> boreans, with whom Perseus, the leader of the people, once
> feasted, having entered their mansions when he came upon
> them sacrificing famous hecatombs of asses to the deity; with
> whose festal banquets and songs of praise Apollo ever is
> especially delighted, and he laughs beholding the rampant
> wantonness of the feasts. And in their habits the muse is not
> an alien from this nation; but everywhere choral bands of
> maidens, and the tones of lyres, and the sounds of flutes are
> agitated, and with the golden laurel having wreathed their
> locks they feast joyously. And neither disease nor destructive
> old age approaches the sacred race; but apart from toils and
> battles they dwell, incurring not the penalty of rigorous
> Nemesis. But breathing forth valour, the son of Danae in
> times past came, and Athena led him to the throng of blessed
> men; and before that he visited the Hyperboreans he slew the
> Gorgon, and came bringing to the islanders the head varie-
> gated with hair of snakes, a strong death. But if the gods
> perform it, nought ever appears to be incredible for me to
> wonder at.[44]

So Perseus, having slain the evil snake-haired monster Gorgon,
was also permitted to visit Hyperborea and enjoy the feasting in
honour of Apollo, following in the 'dragon slaying' path. Pausanias
(*c.* AD 150) describes how the first fruits of the Hyperboreans were
sent to the Greeks:

> At Prasaia is a temple of Apollo. Hither they say are sent the
> first-fruits of the Hyperboreans, and the Hyperboreans are said
> to hand them over to the Arimaspi, the Arimaspi to the Isse-
> dones, from these the Scythians bring them to Sinope, thence
> they are carried by Greeks to Prasaia, and the Athenians take
> them to Delos. The first-fruits are hidden in wheat straw, and
> they are known of none.[45]

So where did the Greeks imagine Hyperborea to be? Diodorus
Siculus describes an account of Hecataeus (*c.* 500 BC):

In the regions beyond the land of the Celts there lies in the ocean an island no smaller than Sicily. This island ... is situated in the North and is inhabited by the Hyperboreans, who are called by that name because they are beyond the point where the north wind (Boreas) blows; and the island is both fertile and productive of every crop, and since it has an unusually temperate climate, it produces two harvests each year. Moreover the following legend is told concerning it: Leto was born on this island, and for that reason Apollo [the son of Zeus and Leto] is honoured among them above all other gods; and the inhabitants are looked upon as priests of Apollo, after a manner, since daily they praise this god continuously in song and honour him exceedingly. And there is also on the island both a magnificent sacred precinct of Apollo and a notable temple which is adorned with many votive offerings and is built after the pattern of the spheres. Furthermore, a city is there which is sacred to this god, and the majority of its inhabitants are players on the cithara; and these continually play on this instrument in the temple and sing hymns of praise to the god, glorifying his deeds ... The account is also that the god visits the island every nineteen years, the period in which the return of the stars to the same place in the heavens in accomplished; and for this reason the nineteen-year period is called by the Greeks 'the year of Meton.[46]

This refers to the 'Metonic cycle' of 18.61 years in which the phases of the moon and the sun correspond, and from which eclipses can be predicted. Consequently many suppose the 'temple of Apollo' to be Stonehenge and the island Britain, because the 56 'Aubrey holes' at Stonehenge could have been used for these predictions (19 + 19 + 18 = 56 years).

Strabo (born 64 or 63 BC) places the land further south and not too far from the Scythians.

On the right, as one sails into the Caspian Sea are those Scythians or Sarmatians, who live in the country contiguous to Europe between the Tanaïs River and this sea; the greater part of them are nomads ... On the left are the Eastern Scythians, also nomads, who extend as far as the Eastern Sea and India.

Now all the peoples towards the north were by the ancient Greek historians given the general name 'Scythians' or 'Celtoscythians', but the writers of still earlier times, making distinctions between them, called those who lived above the Euxine [the Black Sea] and the Ister [Danube] and the Adriatic, 'Hyperboreans, Sauromatians and Arimaspians'.[47]

But Spanuth makes a case for their land being in the region of present-day Jutland, the little island of Heligoland, which he claims was once part of a larger land mass now submerged. Apparently an old name for part of Norway was Halogaland—is there again some confusion? He points out that Pliny in his *Natural History* made a distinction between Britain and the land of the Hyperboreans.[48] In view of certain parallels between Apollo and Freyr as we shall subsequently explore (though not to say that they were one and the same being), the Jutland connection cannot be ruled out. Ultimately it comes down to not being a matter of trying to locate the exact region of Hyperborea, but to understand that there we reach a *state*, rather than a place—a state in which the sun-given life forces abound and can be rightly used again for the service of humanity.

Hyperborea has passed into Norwegian folklore in the form of the legend of Utrøst. It is a place described as being much further north than Britain or Jutland, beyond the Lofoten Islands—Røst being the outermost island there. Sometimes it is pictured as being beneath the sea. Its green meadows both hark back to the sun forces of the etheric and also hint at a future green land of the god Vidar, who survives Ragnarok and of whom we shall speak later. The green land or Greenland was the name given to this idyllic near-polar region. Indeed, up until the early Middle Ages, the island of Greenland was much warmer and supported a significant colony of Norse people. The islands were said to appear and disappear and perhaps were similar to Hy Brasil of the Celts. On Utrøst could be seen fields of gleaming golden barley, the main ingredient for making mead. Strabo comments on the grain fields in the northern land of Thule:

For Thule of all countries that are named, is set farthest north ... [Pytheas] says that, of the animals and domesticated fruits, there is an utter dearth of some and a scarcity of the others, and that the people live on millet and other herbs, and on fruits and roots and where there are grain and honey, the people get their beverage from them. As for the grain, he says, since they have no pure sunshine—they pound it out in large storehouses after first gathering in the ears thither, for the threshing floors become useless because of this lack of sunshine and because of the rains.[49]

This is no legendary land, but a clearly observed northern region. In esoteric language, however, earlier peoples recognized the sun forces—cosmic forces within grain, especially wheat and bread. Anglian kings traced their origin back to Odin/Woden. They also traced one line back to Noah. From him was descended Sceaf, father of Sceld or Skyld, the father of Beowulf. William of Malmesbury describes how Sceaf as a boy appeared on the shore of the island of Scandza [*sic*] asleep in a little boat, his head resting on a sheaf of corn. Hence his name Sceaf—sc pronounced sh in Old English.[50] Of divine origin were the ancient rulers of the Germanic peoples. Right into the twentieth century have the Norwegian people retained a sense of the old connection between sun-ripened grain and divine beings, and the festival of the birth of the sun god at Christmas. Sigrid Undset describes how people in her district of Gudbrandsdal kept the custom of hanging out a sheaf of grain for the midwinter feast of Yule:

It is the custom in Norway to put a sheaf of grain outside the windows at Christmas-time. Thousands of years ago the Stone Age people in Norway, when they had learned to grow grain, believed that the spirit that lived in the earth and made things grow, fled when the grain was cut. It hid, they thought, in the last remaining stalks, and when these had been cut down, this spirit of growth was thought to be imprisoned in them. That was why the peasants laid aside the last sheaf and kept it. In midwinter ... the sun, looking ill and feverishly red, crept up over the edge of the forest to hang low over the earth a short while, before dropping down to hide itself again—then the Stone Age people fetched this last sheaf of grain and hung it near the place they lived. The spirit in it helped the sun become strong again, and once more to warm and light the earth to triumph over evil winter. Then the spirit returned to the thawing fields to bring the people a new harvest of blessed grain.[51]

Apollo's chariot was drawn by swans—a bird associated with sun cults and hence divine kingship. In the Greek spring swans would migrate northwards to return in October. It is normally either a mute bird or, if a whooper swan, makes a braying donkey-like sound. The swans which drew Apollo's chariot were a more northern species called the whistling swan (*Cygnus musicus*). It is this swan that has given rise to the legend that it bursts into song just before its death. There is, however, more than legend to the 'swan song'.

> Wings fixed, he commenced at once his song which was continued until the water was reached nearly a mile away. Never before or since have I heard anything like the song of this stricken swan. It sounded at times like the running notes of an octave, most plaintive in character and musical in tone and, as the sound was borne to us, mellowed by the distance, we stood astounded and could only exclaim 'We have heard the song of a dying swan'. (H.W. Robinson, quoted by Frederick M. Ahl in *Amber, Avallon and Apollo's Singing Swan.*)[52]

Apollo is the god of music. With his seven-string lyre he produces the cosmic harmonies, the music of the spheres—the sounds of the seven planetary spheres. He understands and mediates the secrets of the tone ether. Frederick Ahl draws our attention to a remarkable linguistic connection: 'swan' and *Schwann* derive from an Indo-European root meaning 'sound', cf. Sanscrit *svanas*—'noise'. 'Swan' *is* therefore the 'singing swan'.

Birds are traditionally messengers between the spiritual and the human realm—we can recall Odin's pair of ravens, Hugin and Munin, and Athene's owl. The swan is also a 'messenger' in a stage of initiation. Knights of the Grail worked from the spiritual world once deceased, and the human being with whom they worked was known as a 'swan'—such as Lohengrin, the 'swan knight'.[53] In northern mythology, warriors who met their death nobly on the battlefield were received by a Valkyrie, who was often imagined as a swan maiden. In his initiation, Sigurd-Siegfried united himself with a Valkyrie whilst still alive.[54] Thus swans have a special role in the state of passing through death or initiation—and also with birth. In order to come into birth, we learn how the soul must draw together an etheric body, a life body from the surrounding cosmic ether:

> The etheric body breathes in light, uses up the light and changes it into darkness. It can then receive into this darkness the sound of the cosmos that lives in the harmony of the spheres; can receive into it the impulses of life ... And while the etheric body prepares the light for the darkness and thereby breathes inwardly, it lives in that it receives the sound of the cosmos and changes it into the life of the cosmos. And what we receive in this way as our etheric body comes down to us from the wide and distant spaces of the cosmos at particular times.[55]

Apollo and his swan-borne chariot were not normally connected with birth but Artemis, his twin sister, acted as midwife and could be called upon to assist women in labour. Nonetheless Apollo's ability to bring the music of the spheres down to earth cannot be entirely separated from the incoming soul being borne on the cosmic tone ether. Both are manifestations of creative power.

For the more northern peoples the swan had a special connection to both birth and death (as we saw with the Valkyrie). Bronze Age rock carvings in Norway and along the Baltic coast depict swans and boats, and a bird-ship in connection with solar orbs and wheels. Njord, one of the older Vanir gods, dwelt in the part of Asgard known as Noatun. He much preferred it to the mountainous home of his wife Skadi. He said: 'I hate mountains—not long was I there, just nine nights: wolves howling I thought ugly compared with the swan's song.'[56]

In Norwegian, *svane*—swan could be related to *svanger*—pregnant, for in German pregnancy is *Schwangerschaft*. Thus we are clearly entering into the mysteries of birth. Three goddesses presided over birth in the northern regions—the Norns or carriers of destiny. They tended one of the three roots of Yggdrasil (the northern Tree of Life) by watering it from a nearby well each day. This was 'Urd's well'—*urdabrunnr,* where the gods met daily to hold council. Urd was old and looked back to the past. Her name means 'destiny', *wurd* in old Saxon and *wyrd* in Anglo-Saxon, from which we have the word 'weird'—now meaning simply something uncanny or peculiar. The 'Three Weird Sisters' in *Macbeth* are in fact the Norns, turned into witches, their well now a cauldron, according to Shakespeare, who drew on Holinshed's *Chronicles* (1577–87).

Urd's sisters were Verdandi—'being in the act of becoming', connected to *werden*, to become, and *Werth* or 'worth'. And Skuld—'shall be', or 'necessity', pictured holding an opened scroll. Her name in German becomes *Schuld*—'guilt' or 'debt'. Two swans swam on Urd's well and legend states that all swans have descended from these two. The Norns would also put on swan plumage like the Valkyries. These were, however, goddesses of destiny rather than actual birth or fertility. For the latter, Njord was pictured as having a female aspect—*Nerthus*. The rites of Nerthus and her chariot in what is thought to have been Jutland (Jylland) and elsewhere, also in north Germany, were described by Tacitus:

> [The tribes] share a common worship or Nerthus, or Mother Earth. They believe that she takes part in human affairs, riding in a chariot among her people. On an island of the sea stands an inviolate grove, in which, veiled with a cloth, is a chariot that none but the priest may touch. The priest can feel the presence of the goddess in this holy of holies, and attends her with deepest reverence as her chariot is drawn along by cows. Then follow days of rejoicing and merrymaking in every place that she condescends to visit and sojourn in. No one goes to war, no one takes up arms; every iron object is locked away. Then, and then only, are peace and quiet known and welcomed, until the goddess, when she has had enough of the society of men, is restored to her sacred precinct by the priest. After that, the chariot, the vestments, and (believe it if you will) the goddess herself, are cleansed in a secluded lake. This service is performed by slaves who are immediately afterwards drowned in the lake. Thus mystery begets terror and a pious reluctance to ask what that sight can be which is seen only by men doomed to die.[57]

Rudolf Steiner has likened the experience of Nerthus to the intimation to a mother that a child is to be born to her. In a

Christmas lecture he described how the early tribe of Ingaevones eagerly awaited the first child to be born at Christmas, who would become their chief—births at that time being regulated so that babies were all born close to Christmas-Yule.[58] This must have related to a time hundreds of years before Tacitus, but the custom of the chariot seems to have lingered on in Jutland for a long time. Spanuth suggests that the island on which the Nerthus rites took place was Heligoland—'Hyperborea', which formerly was connected to a larger land mass.[59]

The principal god of the Ingaevones was Ingvi-Freyr. He and his sister Freya were the children of Njord of whom Nerthus was perceived as a female aspect. He was the god of fertility and his rune, when later these came to be inscribed, was the rune Ing ◊, sometimes drawn as ✗ when it could suggest the DNA spiral. The Old English rune poem described Ing and is apparently an echo of the Nerthus mystery, Ing himself being identified with Njord-Nerthus and Ingvi-Freyr his son. The syllable 'Ing' came to be an indicator of belonging to a particular tribe, e.g. Heard -ingas, Hard -ing:

> Ing was first seen by the men of the East Danes. Later he went eastwards. Across the waves he strode, and his chariot followed after. So the Heardingas named the hero.[60]

The diamond-shaped rune may just be a decoration now, but it appears on the roof of the restored wheat barn at Temple Cressing in Essex, where it once belonged to a Templar Preceptory. The fertility of wheat and barley, which we have already seen in the stories of Sceaf and of Utrøst, had to be maintained also.

Njord-Nerthus -Ing as a messenger of birth can therefore be seen as a kind of counterpart of the Greek Apollo. We should not automatically suppose one god is the same as another from a different culture, but there are nevertheless certain connections we can make. Apollo, as we saw, was a god connected with the sun, who went to his ancient northerly home each autumn. He was also a kind of dragon-slayer, overcoming the vapours of the dragon or python, which arose through a cleft in the earth at Delphi. He shone on the

Pythia, conquering unruly passions and she became a sibyl and spoke his oracles. Because of this he is sometimes identified as the Archangel Michael. Michael and the earthly St George bear resonances with Apollo, but we should be clear that he is not the same spiritual being. Before Christ came to earth and entered a human body he performed a certain deed in the spiritual world, permeating an angelic being in order that harmful forces could be driven from the human soul, so that thinking, feeling and willing might be harmonized. The angelic being had to connect himself with the dragon nature.[61] This Angel-like being later became the child Jesus as described in St Luke's Gospel, often called the 'Nathan Jesus' because of his genealogy as recounted there. It was a soul that had not descended to earth before but was held in its state of innocence and purity in the spiritual world until the birth of Jesus.[62] Everything this child did was an expression of purest love. In a similar way to Nerthus visiting the souls of the pre-Christian Ingaevones, the Archangel Gabriel visits Mary to inform her of the coming child. The Ingaevones had a special feeling for the child of St Luke's Gospel.

> So in contemplating in the Luke Gospel the story of how the Archangel Gabriel appears to Mary, we may seek its origin in the true visions which occurred in what was later mirrored in the Nerthus Mystery with its symbols. This had migrated over to the East.[63]

Apollo was a healer god, bringing harmony with his music. Because later Greeks sometimes pictured their gods in amorous associations with earthly women as a kind of mistaken, Luciferically inspired reflection of their interaction with human beings, it does not blot out the much loftier identity of Apollo.

The incoming soul, born on the tone ether, was to bear something even finer. We explained the four ethers at the beginning of the first chapter. When mentioning the tone (chemical) ether we can understand that the 'music of the spheres' is more than metaphor, as planetary forces are behind individual tones, which the movement art of eurythmy can reveal. When Rudolf Steiner lectured in Torquay in 1924, he spoke of the dangers and possible misuse particularly of the chemical ether radiations.[64] One way of looking at this is to recall that at the 'fall' of humanity, 'eating of the Tree of Life' was forbidden to human beings. Steiner explained that the 'Tree of Knowledge' corresponds to the use of the warmth and light ethers that were permitted to humanity, corresponding to will (warmth/fire) and feeling (light) being freely accessible on an immediate personal level. The two 'higher' ethers, life and sound (chemical)—the 'Tree of Life'—were withheld in the sense they were to be inaccessible to human will. Steiner makes the connection of these two with meaning (life ether) and thinking (sound ether), which may seem puzzling. It may help to reflect that for thinking to have a direct effect on a person or substance, an act of magic usually has to take place involving the use of physical substances, sound, etc., or alternatively, overpowering someone with hypnosis, which is also related to a manipulation of the etheric. This is one way in which these forces can be abused as they also thus harness elemental beings. However, humanity will gradually be granted the rightful use of these higher ethers more and more in the future if people can connect to the power of Christ. For it was when the Christ Being entered the carefully prepared 'Nathan' Jesus body at the baptism in the River Jordan that these higher ethers were returned to humanity as a future potential. Christ is described by St John as the *Logos* or *Word*, carrying both the nature of 'sound' and 'meaning'—the divine creative cosmic word.[65]

> In the beginning was the Word, and the Word was with God, and the Word was God. He was in the beginning with God; all things were made through Him, and without Him was not anything made that was made. In Him was life, and the life was the light of men. The light shines in the darkness, and the darkness has not overcome it.

The true mystery of Apollo is thus revealed. His seven-stringed lyre was able to 'play' the creative cosmic music as the Nathan Jesus body bore the Christ. The planetary forces behind this 'music' were expressed through Christ at every moment of his three-year time on earth. Unlike an ordinary human horoscope fixed at the time of birth, Christ could express the cosmic patterns continuously as he lived and moved on earth in the Holy Land.[66] That the early Christians had a feeling for Apollo in connection with the sun and

Christ is shown by the earliest Christian sculptures drawing on the pagan representations of Apollo in order to portray Jesus. Significantly, after Christianity became the official religion of the Roman Empire, Jupiter/Zeus gradually became the preferred model—bearded, majestic, enthroned as an image of temporal rulership and power rather than of love and healing.

In the human body the head bears the greatest concentration of these two ethers, with light/air in the middle —rhythmic system and warmth/fire in the metabolism and will. Thus the head corresponds to the 'most northerly region' of humans and Apollo carries rejuvenating forces back and forth. This will be explored further in the chapter on Thule.

3. The Druids and Odinic Mysteries

The general view is that the period of the older Vanir gods in northern mythology, such as Njord, Freyr and Freya, correspond to that of the Celtic/Druidic period of the third post-Atlantean epoch. The coming of the *Aesir* would then correspond to the fourth epoch which began in 747 BC.[67] The 'battle' between the two families of gods would be the overcoming of the earlier epoch. We shall see how this was experienced in the northern kingdoms. The god Heimdall, also of the Vanir, created the three castes of nobility, independent farmers and serfs and then returned to become a guardian at the Bifrost Bridge leading from Midgard (the human world) to Asgard, the home of the gods. We are about to explore the coming of Odin/ Wotan of the Aesir, a being who should have become a Spirit of Form (Exusiai) but held back as an Archangel in order to accompany human development. Beings who create language are really Spirits of Form who have held themselves back as a sacrifice. At around this time of the start of the fourth epoch, the larynx and brain formations altered. It may be one reason why Odin came to be imagined as a historical figure. The Celtic/Druidic peoples 'heard' nature speak through sound—music and song, whereas the northern peoples were to 'perceive' forms—runic forms visually.[68]

When speaking about the Druids in later lectures, Rudolf Steiner introduces a connection with the Odinic mysteries which are not found in either mythological writings or in ordinary scholarship. The Druid culture of the north and west contained an ability to see into nature's processes and the beings working there, but had no form of writing. The Ogham script appeared much later, perhaps around the time of Julius Caesar, and may well derive from the mystery of which we are about to discuss—the runic script. The runes are the old Germanic alphabet in which the letters have a meaning in themselves (as with Hebrew). The word is connected with *raunen*, 'to whisper a secret'. The Germanic myths tell how Odin was granted understanding of them when he hung on the World Tree, Yggdrasil, for nine nights, pierced with a spear and deprived of food and drink, until given the intoxicating mead of Odrerir he passed into a state of shamanic ecstasy.

> I know that I hung   on a windy tree
> nine long nights,
> wounded with a spear,   dedicated to Odin
> myself to myself,
> on that tree   of which no man knows
> from where its roots run.
>
> No bread did they give me   or drink from a horn,
> downwards I peered;
> I took up the runes,   screaming I took them,
> then I fell back from there.
>
> Nine mighty spells   I learnt from the famous son
> of Bolthor, Bestla's father,
> and I got a drink   of the precious mead,
> poured from Odrerir.[69]

By hanging on the World Tree Odin was connecting himself with the cosmic ether—if imagined as a human being, his own etheric body would have been partly drawn out from the physical in order to receive the higher wisdom.

After that the letters were not immediately taught to everyone as writing is today, but remained the closely guarded magical-mystery knowledge of the few, the priesthood and the *valas* or *volupsas*— female priestesses or seers. As if to mark the fact that the runes derive from the World Tree, the Tree of Life, they were commonly engraved in wood, especially when used for casting lots. Later they came to be written on stone and metal and eventually used for more everyday purposes. Tacitus described the method used by the Germanic tribes *c.* AD 98:

> For omens and the casting of lots they have the highest regard. Their procedure in casting lots is always the same. They cut off a branch of a nut-bearing tree and slice it into strips; these they mark with different signs and throw them completely at random onto a white cloth. The priest of the state, if the consultation is a public one, or the father of the family if it is private, offers a prayer to the gods, and looking up at the sky picks up three strips, one at a time, and reads their meaning from the signs previously scored on them.[70]

By cutting off a living branch they would have been using 'live wood'—still containing etheric force. Though this method of rune casting is one still used today, the wood is no longer 'alive' and is often replaced by inscribed stones. The method can be recognized in the word 'spell'. To 'spell' is to put the letters of a word in the right order. A 'spell' is an older word for a thin strip of wood—also called a 'spill'; a 'speld' is a splinter, and the game 'spelicans ' or 'spillikins' was originally played with thin pieces of wood. And a 'spell' is of course a magical act. The Gospels are 'Godspell'—God's holy word or 'good tidings'. The writer of the Saxon gospel, the *Heliand*, uses 'spell' for the sacred sayings of Christ, such as the Lord's Prayer. The life forces of the Tree of Life can still reach us today in our language. In German, the word for letter of the alphabet is *Buch-staben* or 'beech stave', an even closer reminder of the nut-bearing tree—also we have *Buch* (beech—book). Nature first wrote the runes, then Odin and finally human beings could read them.

> Runes will you find,   and rightly read,
> of wondrous weight
> of mighty magic,
> which that dyed the dread god,
> which that made the holy hosts,
> and were etched by Odin.[71]

The mystery of writing was taught by Hermes to the Greeks, or Thoth to the Egyptians. Hermes-Mercury was recognized as of a similar nature to Odin/Wotan/Woden, as shown in the name of his day of the week—Wednesday, *Wodnesdaeg, Mercredi*. The spiritual source comes from the inspiration of spirit beings of the planet Mercury (or Buddhi). Buddhi in spiritual science is an older term for the spiritual counterpart to the etheric life processes and for the transformed human etheric body of the future—the Life Spirit. The Archangels are those beings who are at the stage now of perfecting their etheric bodies into Buddhi or Life Spirit. Recalling that Odin who held himself back as a Spirit of Form was active as an Arch-angel makes the whole connection clearer.

According to H.P. Blavatsky, Buddha was inspired by a Spirit of Movement working from the sphere of Mercury—Buddha reached the stage of Buddhahood at the age of 29 whilst 'sitting under the

Bodhi tree'. Steiner confirms this in a lecture of 13 April 1912 in Helsinki.[72] Spirits of Movement (Dynamis) are active in inspiring much longer periods of civilization than would normally be covered by a spirit of the age or Time Spirit (Archai). Partially incorporated in Buddha also was that spirit who had renounced moving forward to a higher stage of development and had remained as an Archangel (i.e. in the sphere of Mercury)—Odin/Wotan.[73] Spirits of Movement are normally associated with the sphere of Mars. These two influences in the gentle Buddha may seem puzzling, but Buddhism has traditionally been the religion of many Asian peoples who have a strong warrior cult. Likewise for the Germanic peoples it was Odin who was also the warrior god, rather than Tyr/Tiw, whose name comes to us in 'Tuesday' (*Mardi*). Speech as a divine creative force also comes from the beings of the sphere of Mars, and Odin was experienced in the breathing and speech—as language. Jakob Streit suggests that the 'green men' to be found carved in many churches are speaking/breathing creative language forces rather than simply vegetation, as a carving of Odin with outpouring streams in the church at Hurum, Norway, is remarkably similar.[74] We have seen, too, that the 'written' source of language was indeed vegetation!

> Nordic man experienced the activity of Odin at a time when he was still in the process of giving the gift of language to the incarnating soul of man.[75]

Odin had undergone another initiation by drinking the magic draught of the gods from the well of Mimir who, it is suggested, was the son of Bolthor referred to in Odin's chant. To receive this mystery wisdom he had to sacrifice one eye—in the myths about him he is depicted as a one-eyed god wearing a broad-brimmed hat. In fact this eye was the 'third eye' of clairvoyance, active in earlier times and connected to the pineal gland. Its function has changed during the course of evolution. To attain higher ego-filled consciousness Odin had to sacrifice the earlier dreamy clairvoyant consciousness. This gift he bestowed on humanity. Yggdrasil means the 'gallows of Ygg' or the Ego, *ich, ic* (Old English), I. It was the Spirits of Form (Exusiai) who implanted the ego in human beings.

Buddha, *c.* 500 BC, came to teach love and compassion and saw the earth as a place of sorrow and pain, a very different kind of spirituality from that inspired by Odin partially incorporated in Sieg or Sigge, said to be a prince of the nomadic Scythian peoples then dwelling in the region of the Black Sea. Buddha would later have to make another sacrifice in order to being peace to the warlike Mars spirits, but before that spiritual event of the early seventeenth century he inspired a mystery centre also in the region of the Black Sea during the seventh and eighth centuries AD.[76] The Buddhism taught there was now strongly permeated by the power of Christ and brought a moral healing force into Europe.

The earlier figure of Sieg, though fierce and brave, was not without some qualities of love, for in the story of Sigurd, when he has come to know 'the speech of the birds', he must surely understand the cosmic love which dwells in birdsong. Now he must experience human love. After the slaying of the dragon Fafnir, Sigurd hears the titmice say:

> A Valkyrie rests   on the rock in sleep
> Flickering fire   flames about her
> With the sleep-thorn Ygg   her erst did prick
> Other heroes she felled   than he had willed.[77]

This is the Valkyrie Brunnhilde or Sigdrifa as she is also called, who was sent to sleep by Ygg-Odin by pricking her with a thorn. As with Sleeping Beauty this implies the magical use of the rune *thorn* Þ ▶ as well. Evidently she had claimed more heroes than Odin thought due to her. Sleeping Beauty is a version of the Sigurd story. At her birth she is visited by twelve 'fairies'—the twelve helpers of the three Norns of fate (one for each zodiac sign no doubt). Beauty is pricked by a magical sleep thorn and awakened by a prince. Sigurd awakens Brunnhilde who teaches him rune magic. He falls in love with her:

> Thy loving counsel   I lief would have
> as long as my life doth last.[78]

Their love bond he forsakes in the further involvement with Gudrun, whom he is tricked into marrying by her mother Grimhild. He forgets Brunnhilde and goes to woo her for Gudrun's brother Gunnar. He has to ride through the ring of fire with which she has surrounded herself. As she arrives to marry Gunnar, Sigurd suddenly recognizes her. A 'karmic knot' has arisen, of tangled relationships. Out of hurt pride Brunnhilde plots to bring about Sigurd's death. In the *Niebelunglied* version she reveals Siegfried's vulnerable spot between his shoulder blades—'*the place where later the Cross will be laid*'.[79] The fiery passionate love of Sigurd and Brunnhilde must pass through the stage of loss and sorrow—it echoes the loss of clairvoyance and the struggle to find one's higher soul nature.

The principal planetary Archangels act also as spirits ruling periods of time of about 330 years. The Archangel of Mercury is Raphael, whose rulership period was AD 850–1180.[80] During this time there was a Mercurial-Odinic flowering of language and literature in the regions to which the Germanic peoples had spread. King Alfred's court in England, the Frankish court of Charlemagne, courts of Ireland, Scotland and Burgundy all attracted the finest poets or 'skalds'. The sagas of Sigurd-Siegfried, Helgi, Beowulf and other heroes were told and sung around fires in the great halls accompanied by plenty of mead drinking. The skalds accompanied the leaders and spun heroic sagas in specific poetic forms, making use of 'kennings' or metaphors. It was believed these had also been taught by spiritual or elemental beings:

> Sky it's called among men,   home of the planets by the gods,
> wind-weaver the Vanir call it,
> the giants call it the world above,   the elves the lovely roof,
> and dwarfs the dripping hall.[81]

Raphael-Mercury is the archangelic spirit of healing, and this branch of Odin's knowledge should not be forgotten. The Old English *Nine Herbs Charm* happily blends pagan and Christian dragon-slaying belief:

> These nine have power against nine poisons.
> A worm came crawling, it bit a man.
> Then Woden took nine glory-twigs,
> smote the adder so that it split into nine.
> There ended Apple and poison
> that she nevermore would enter her house.
>
> . . .

Christ stood over disease of every kind.
I alone know running water
where the nine adders look upon it close.
May all the weeds now spring up herbs,
seas dissolve, all salty water,
when I blow this poison from thee.[82]

The nine herbs were mugwort, plantain, lamb's cress, cockspur grass, camomile, nettle, crab apple, chervil and fennel.

The charm with its knowledge of plant properties and its mention of the adders reminds us again of the Druids. References to 'worm' (not the harmless earthworm variety but meaning a snake or dragon), and 'adder' also suggest harmful earth currents and the old Druid knowledge of how these were connected with moon forces. From Rudolf Steiner we learn that the Druid culture remained dominant in north and west Europe without knowledge of writing, until sometime between 1000 and 600 BC the art of writing runes was brought from a mystery centre in the region of the Black Sea by those who had become initiated into the Mercury mysteries and were servants of Odin/Wotan. The Druids resisted this new culture and thought it intellectual and harmful, a sign of disease, and they tried to treat with medicine anyone who showed signs of succumbing to it.[83] How are we to understand this, of which there is no real trace in historical records nor any actual rune script discovered so early?

The Icelandic Snorri Sturluson writing in the thirteenth century gives two differing accounts of the origins of the Norse peoples. In both, however, Odin and the other Norse deities appear in human form, and not apparently divine. (Christianity had reached Iceland by this time.) In the prologue to the Prose Edda,[84] 'Odin' is descended from Priam, King of Troy. Priam lived about 1190 BC. If we allow 20–30 years for a generation and follow the genealogy through, 'Odin' would be alive in about 700 BC. The other account is at the beginning of the Ynglinga Saga in the *Heimskringla* or 'Norse Kings' Saga'.[85] The Yngling family is traced back to 'Odin', a warrior king living in a city called Asgaard in Asia, or Asaheim. He comes to fight with the people of 'Vanaland' near the Black Sea. He had twelve temple priests called *Drotner*. This sounds familiar. The other Norse gods and goddesses all have a role in the saga which tells of their travelling westward to settle in Scandinavia and northern Europe. There is no mention of Priam of Troy. In the Prose Edda version one of Odin's sons, Veggdegg (is this Vidar, of whom we shall hear more later?), is given East Saxony to rule. Beldegg or Baldur was given Westphalia. In this region we find the mystery centre of the Externsteine, around which the spiritual centre of 'Asgard' could once be found, according to Rudolf Steiner's research—more about this later.

Such sagas were not unusual in the Middle Ages. In this case they attempt to give an exoteric account, perhaps from differing viewpoints of what we learn as the spiritual reality from Steiner: that Odin was partly incorporated in human form, the Scythian Sieg. Snorri was a Christian, and like many other medieval scholars, thought that the pagan gods were actually historical figures whom ignorant folk worshipped as gods.

The Scythians were a nomadic peoples, possibly from Asia, who settled in southern Russia, the Crimea and the shores of the Black Sea around 800 BC.[86] They were warlike and without a script. They produced finely decorated objects for everyday use. The style passed westwards and is believed to have influenced later Celtic and Viking styles with their intricately woven forms of animals and elemental beings, which were no doubt still visible to the people then. (According to Geoffrey of Monmouth's *History of the Kings of Britain*[87] and also *The Anglo-Saxon Chronicle*,[88] the Picts who settled in Scotland round about the first century AD came from Scythia—but historians do not appear to agree on the origin of the Picts). A sub-group of the Scythians were the Sarmatians, from whom descended the Ossetians—still to be found in the region of the Caucasus and speaking an Indo-Germanic language. An Ossetian legend described the birth of a boy born to a woman who was stunned by a thunderbolt and died. The people caring for the child called him Ud-dæn, meaning 'I am the soul'. He grew up to discover bronze smelting and the forging of weapons, and then departed northwards in search of women with long golden hair. Arriving in Scandinavia he was hailed as a god and married a king's daughter. Ud-dæn or Odin later returned to the Causasus, leaving his son Votan in Scandinavia. The hill where he was buried was first known as 'Odin's Hill' and later 'Christ's Hill'.[89]

The shores of Thrace and the Black Sea were also populated with colonies from Greek islands and Ionian cities by the sixth century BC. There was a flourishing trade of amber, furs and skins, also with the Goths who may have been the Getes (Getae) from Gotland and the Baltic regions, who came down the valley of the Dnieper to the Black Sea and the Danube. Between 540 and 480 BC the Ionian and Greek island alphabet bore a remarkable similarity to the later runic alphabet. Isaac Taylor in *Greeks and Goths. A Study on the Runes*[90] has shown this, and gives the clearest history of the origin of the runes and of the later Celtic Ogham script. For instance:

Thracian	**Runic**		
l lambda	⌐ lagu		L
	ᚱ rad		R
M mu	ᛗ man		M
Σ sigma	ᚴ sigil		S
l iota	ı ls		l
Ω omega	ᛟ othal		O
X chi	× gyfu		G
k Thracian gamma	ᚲ ken		K or C

This is earlier than the connection many scholars make between the runes and the inscriptions in the Etruscan alphabet found on 26 bronze helmets dating from the fourth century BC. The Goths later developed the Gothic Futhark and a more cursive script. The Common Germanic or Elder Futhark (as above) of 24 runes has not been found inscribed on anything dating earlier than about AD 200, thus Taylor's theory has been overlooked in favour of a later origin, probably Roman, for the runes. It is too detailed a subject to go into here, but Taylor's theory of a common northern Greek-Gothic origin dating back to the sixth or seventh centuries BC is strikingly close to Steiner's statement that Sieg (Odin) brought the runic script westwards at that time. We have to remember that its usage would almost have certainly been restricted to the priesthood and not to the ordinary people to etch their names on their combs as happened much later. Anything inscribed at that time was almost certainly destroyed as it was too 'magical'. Tacitus in his *Germania, c.* AD 98 nevertheless refers to 'lot casting' which was presumably runic divination. As the strips were scored with signs, this suggests that a 'protected' writing had already begun by the first century AD. One method of rune casting is to throw nine twigs onto a cloth and see which runes appear in the pattern formed. This could have been the earliest kind of rune spread—the letters and their associations deriving from the perceived *form* (as stated earlier), and the possible clairvoyant images that arose from it. As an activity of will, Steiner speaks of this method as the expression of looking for a sign or token, which can be discerned lying behind the northern European style of painting in the Renaissance, a much later perception of form.[91] On another more 'esoteric' note, the Elder Futhark is divided into three series of eight runes, or *aetts. Aett* or eight is 8, the lemniscate form of the Mercury staff, thus revealing a Woden-Mercury connection.

The Ogham script has been found especially in the west of England, south Wales and Ireland where there were also Scandinavian settlers, possibly Jutes from Jutland. It uses a 'branch' or 'twig' form and Taylor demonstrates how it most likely arose from the runic alphabet. He suggests, too, that the names of the alphabet *Bethluisnion* also derive from the runes, e.g:

Ogham	Runic	
beith	beorc	b
suil	sigil	s
duir	tyr	t
muin	man	m

Like the 'spells' from Yggdrasil, the *Bethluisnion* with its tree names (see for instance Robert Graves, *The White Goddess*)[92] shows how the letters derive from the living forces of the Tree of Life. The Druids evidently permitted the sacred sounds revealed to them by tree spirits (Beth, Beorc = Birch; Luis = rowan; Nion = ash) to be written down eventually. Graves' account of the alphabet is very detailed, linking many mythologies in a rather tortuous way, but his main thesis of a Spirit Being residing in the forces of nature, the Great Goddess, or 'Sophia', the 'wisdom of creation' is in keeping with our theme.

As befits both Druidic and Norse spirituality, the rowan or mountain ash, found growing naturally more in northern England and Scotland, gets its name from Norwegian *raun,* connected with the German word *raunen* to whisper, and *runa,* charm or rune (Old Norse *rún*). The rowan par excellence is a magical tree. Its country names include witch-wood, witchen, wicken, wiggin, quicken, quickbeam, which show its importance in warding off evil spells and being connected with the Tree of Life.[93] It is found near stone circles and there were sacred rowan thickets in Rügen and on Baltic amber islands.

> In Iceland, the legend of the sacred rowan tree tells of how, around the winter solstice, a rowan tree becomes radiant, every branch glowing with an unearthly light, which no stormy wind can extinguish.[94]

Perhaps Yggdrasil was a *mountain* ash?

Odin was the chief of the Aesir gods. Often called Valfather—All-father (he had 50 other names as well), but Snorri's Sturluson's *Edda* tells of the earlier race of gods, the Vanir—chiefly Njord, his son Freyr and daughter Freya. At first the Aesir fought with the Vanir, but later a truce was agreed. The Vanir gods sent their two foremost male gods, Njord and Freyr (though earlier, Njord was perceived as androgynous), as hostages, and the Aesir sent Hoenir and Mimir. Hoenir was very silent and the Vanir did not think this fair exchange so they cut off Mimir's head and sent it to the Aesir. Odin chanted runic spells over it and learned more secrets from it. The battle between Aesir and Vanir is said by Ernst Uehli and others to indicate the Germanic peoples overcoming the Celtic—the fourth post-Atlantean epoch taking over from the third.[95] They perceived the working of Angels and Archangels as the Aesir—the principal beneficent ones, as opposed to the divine beings of earlier times—the Vanir. Whether the Odin mysteries reached the British

Isles earlier than the period of the Germanic migrations is hard to say. One can imagine there was some contact, even if it was repelled at first. What later is done by 'ordinary' people is usually foreshadowed by the deeds of initiates. The Odin initiate, however, first established his mystery centre in the region of the Teutoburg Forest near Paderborn in Germany, where the remarkable 'Externsteine' are to be found today. This mystery centre (of which more later) is still a potent place to visit, with its curiously shaped rocks rising out of the forest clearing, its stone altar at the top of one of the rocks reached by what once was probably a rope bridge so that the initiates had to acquire the necessary courage to sway dizzily about 120 feet above ground before they could experience the sun god at the summer solstice, and with its hollowed-out caves experience the 'hunt for Baldur'—the winter solstice mystery of the sun at midnight. Rudolf Steiner describes how this region was the spiritual focus for the whole Germanic aspect of the northern mysteries.

> In the eyes of the world it would be regarded as the height of folly to speak of that spiritual centre on the continent of Europe which at one time radiated the most powerful impulses, the centre which the seat of exalted Spirits before the Celtic Folk Spirit as Celtic Archangel had established a new centre in the High Castle of the Grail ... It must seem the height of folly, as I said, if we were to indicate as the central source of inspiration for the various Germanic tribes, that district which now lies over central Germany—not actually on the Earth, but hovering above it. If you were to describe an arc to include the towns of Detmold and Paderborn, you would then delimit the region from where the most exalted Spirits were sent on their several missions to Northern and Western Europe. Hence, because the great centre of spiritual inspiration was situated here, legend tells of Asgard having been actually located at this place on earth ... in later years its spiritual mission was taken over by the Castle of the Grail.[96]

It may sound like a reversal of what we have just said, that the spiritual Grail mystery took over from the mystery centre of Asgard, as the former is usually connected more with earlier Celtic mythology rather than Germanic. But in these lectures Rudolf

Steiner is talking about the *esoteric* mission of the Celtic peoples, how their Folk Spirit or Archangel became the leader of esoteric Christianity, having renounced the role of Folk Spirit. Thus the Celts declined as a nation and became absorbed into the Germanic culture of the Anglo-Saxons and Franks, apart from those in the western regions of the British Isles, France and Ireland who still struggle to maintain a separate identity from out of a longing for their past glory. However, 'Celtic' Christians continued their mission by enabling their special spirituality to flow into Christianity. This took the form of, more exoterically, the Celtic Church of the early Christian centuries whose wealth of spiritual insight was later suppressed by the Roman Church spreading from the south, but not before it had taken its spiritual treasure to the continent of Europe and Scandinavia, as will be explored. The medieval Grail legends are one echo of this.

The interweaving of these strands is like the Celtic-Germanic braided decorative patterns.

4. Thule and the Thul

Hopefully by now we can separate our associations of Thule from the Thule Gesellschaft. In fact these myths of an 'Aryan' homeland and a Golden Age have been very well explored by Jocelyn Godwin in his book *Arktos. The Polar Myth in Science, Symbolism and Nazi Survival*[97] and the whole political racist connection in Nicholas Goodrick-Clarke's *The Occult Roots of Nazism*. My intention is not to cover this painful ground and explore all of it again, but to bring to bear other aspects in line with history, northern mythology and spiritual science.

The Greeks, as already stated, believed Thule to be a real land and it is helpful to look further at some of these ideas as they have a bearing on early sea voyages, which are one of many strands we have in order to show the capacities of pre-Renaissance explorers and their possible secret knowledge. We mentioned that Pytheas of Massilia sailed west and north at about the time Alexander the Great was marching east to India. Pytheas studied the stars and made very accurate measurements; he was a little younger than Aristotle and was of his more scientific frame of mind. He sailed round Britain, north to the Shetlands, to 'Orcas' in the North Sea, apparently north of the Shetlands rather than the Orkneys (Orcades). He claimed to have visited Thule, then sailed back to Heligoland to collect amber, a profitable trade then. He stated that Thule was a six-day voyage from Britain northwards—two days from Scotland to the Shetlands, and four days to 'Thule'. He claimed to have reached Arctic waters a day from Thule. Pytheas' own writings are unfortunately lost and we have to rely on Strabo or Pliny quoting him. So Thule has been identified with both Iceland and Norway. It is even suggested that Pytheas did not go there himself but learned about it at Orcas, for the name Thule was already known to the Greeks variously as *Thula, Thyle, Thile, Thila, Tyle, Tila*.[98] The nineteenth-century explorer Richard Burton is quoted as saying:

> Some derive Thule from the Arabic word Tule ... which signified 'afar off', the poets usually call it 'Ultima Thule' ... but I

rather prefer the reason of the name given by the learned Bochartus, who makes it to be Phoenician, and affirms that it signifies 'darkness' in that language. 'Thule' in the Tyrian tongue was 'a shadow' whence it is commonly used to signify 'darkness' and the island Thule is as much as to say an 'island of darkness'. Or it may mean 'obscurity.[99]

This does not quite fit with a land of light and everlasting life but is an interesting observation in that Thule has acquired a 'shadow' side. Professor Björn Collinder, a Swedish philologist thinks the name comes from the same stem as Old Norse *thaul, thaularvagr*, a bay in which one can get locked—Thule, land of narrow bays, the Norwegian coast. Another suggestion is that it was an old Celtic name for Iceland. The Venerable Bede wrote of travellers going to Ireland from there and thought Thule was Iceland, as did Dicuil in AD 825, Adam of Bremen in 1075, Saxo Grammaticus in the twelfth century, Columbus and others later. Procopius on the other hand, in the sixth century AD thought Thule was Norway, as did the explorer Nansen. He thought Iceland was too far to reach in six days and that currents would have swept Pytheas towards Norway. But people forget the speed of the Greek rowers. The name 'Norway' does mean the 'north way'. Brögger suggests Bronze Age peoples sailed northern oceans from Cape Finisterre to south-west England, and across the North Sea to south-west Norway, to Scotland via Shetland and the Orkneys and probably to America also, and that navigation *declined* during the Iron Age until Viking times. There was flourishing trade between England and the Mediterranean from *c.* 2000–1400 BC; trade then diverted more towards Scandinavia. From 1000 BC it swung back towards Cornwall. Peoples in the South Seas have made even longer voyages with more primitive equipment. The Inuit in skin kayaks could brave very rough icy seas, and if people could sail to Iceland and Norway from Scotland in those pre-Viking times they could have reached Greenland and Newfoundland also.

Thule has also been likened to Atlantis, the submerged continent of ancient times, but this fits far less well than Hyperborea, the Golden Age of paradise, where unfallen ether forces were concentrated. However, it is not as fruitful to try and identify it with

any particular region as to look at Thule as a state of 'being'.
Connected to 'Thule' we find the term *thul, thyle (Þule)*, meaning
variously a sage, a bard, a spokesperson. In the Old English poem
Beowulf, we read:

> Swylce Þær UnferÞ <u>Þyle</u>
> æt fotum sœt frean Scyldinga

> Also there Unferth spokesman
> At feet sat of lord of Scyldings[100]

> (John Porter's literal translation, but lost in Seamus Heaney's.
> Much as I might wish to retain the spelling using the Old
> English letter *thorn* Þ for 'th', in the interests of clarity it will
> be 'th'.)

The thul was a poet—a skald or scop, associated with the courts
of a king or jarl, but there are suggestions that he was more than
that—that he was in fact a shamanic individual who had conquered
not the Arctic regions but himself, and visited the otherworld.

> In the Northern tradition, those who underwent magical seers'
> journeys—sages and inspired orators—were called Thul or
> Thyle. Thule is a Norse place name which means 'the place
> where one is forced to turn back'. It is also the name of the
> mythical land of the north, beyond which it is not possible to
> venture. A Thul is a person who has journeyed to the other-
> world, and turned back again to this one. His or her symbol is
> the Thorn rune.[101] Þ, ᚦ

The first stage of a pupil in the Odin mystery initiation was of
purification or catharsis—the pupil was a 'dragon-slayer'. Sigurd-
Siegfried was called 'Fafnir's slayer' (Fafnir being the dragon), and
'Loddfafnir' is a name for a pupil who had reached this stage. Thus
he is addressed in the *Havamal* or the 'Sayings of Har, the Wise
One':

> Tis time to chant   on the sage's [thul's] chair:
>   at the well of Urd
> I saw but said naught   I saw and thought,
>   (listened to Har's lore)

Of runes I heard men speak   unravelling them,
 At the hall of Har,
 In the hall of Har
 And so I heard them say:

Hear you, Loddfafnir,   and heed it well
 Learn it, 'twill lend you strength
 Follow it, 'twill further you:
in a witch's arms   beware of sleeping
 linking your limbs with hers . . .[102]

So a thul must also be a dragon-slayer. One of Odin's many names was Fimbulthul, thus he, having mastered the runes, was a chief thul. In the 'Lay of Vafthrudnir' Odin tests his wisdom against the giant Vafthrudnir and is addressed thus:

 (Odin said)
Gagnrath my name;   as guest I come
 To your threshold thirsty, oh thurs!
Needful of welcome   I wandered long
 To your hearth hither I fared.

 (Vafthrudnir said)
Why then, Gagnrath,   greet me from floor?
 In the hall seat you on settle!
Moot then may we   who most knows
 Whether guest or grizzled thul.[103]

Seamus Heaney may not have translated 'thul' literally, but in his introduction to *Beowulf* he refers to another word which may be linked, the Old English *Þolian* (*tholian*), meaning 'to suffer'. One cannot become a true thul without passing through suffering.[104]

In earlier times the bard, poet—thul—held in memory the history of the tribe or peoples and could sing or recite it. The thul spoke *thulur,* alliterative mnemonic poetry with a magical-religious content, which guarded these traditions. Whether there were female *thulir* (plural) is uncertain. Certainly there were the *Vala,* or *Volva* (cf. *Veleda,* a particular Germanic seeress), prophetesses, sibyls, seers, who knew their rune magic and who could chant or sing but did not necessarily have the same role as the thul. The female seers retained their magic powers well into Christian times—see the fascinating description of Thorbjorg, the 'Little Sibyl', in the Icelandic 'Eirik's Saga' (Chapter 4).[105] She is treated with great respect—evidently pagan customs continued acceptably within the new Christian practices at this period. As we saw with the meaning of 'spell', for a long time after Christ there remained the sense for words having a magical power and for certain people who were gifted with godly forces being able to make use of them.

Until more recent, prosaic times the idea of a poet seized by a state of ecstasy or being divinely inspired was not so unusual. Stephen Coote, writing of John Keats, says that Keats had the belief of the poet as a kind of shaman, both priest and doctor.[106] Keats's 'god' was Apollo—god of poetry and healing. Keats had trained as a surgeon (a much simpler profession in his day) before devoting his short life to writing, so it is perhaps not surprising that the thul has descendents. (However, the Norse god of poetry was actually Bragi, from whom we get the word 'to brag'!)

Keats wrote both an ode and a hymn to Apollo:

> God of the golden bow,
>   And of the golden lyre,
> And of the golden hair,
>   And of the golden fire.
>   Charioteer
>   Of the patient year,
>   Where—where slept thine ire,
> When like a blank idiot I put on thy wreath,
>   Thy laurel, thy glory,
>   The light of thy story,
> Or was I a worm—too low crawling, for death?
>   O Delphic Apollo![107]

Keats describes himself here as a 'blank idiot'—one cannot help wondering if the 'fool' with all its connotations of entertaining the king or nobleman, and also of being on a spiritual journey, is not in some way connected with both the concept and the word 'thul'. He, too, carries a kind of staff of Mercury.

We have been trying to indicate that to visit 'Thule' was not necessarily to sail into northern waters but to enter a more mystical, inspired state in which one might hear the voice of a divine being and be able to bring this forth in a magical or artistic form. We could mention many inspired poets—Rainer Maria Rilke experienced what seems to have been an angelic encounter and thus the *Duino Elegies* were composed. Whilst staying with his patron and friend, Princess Marie Thurn und Taxis-Hohenlohe at Duino, he was walking on the battlements in a strong wind when he seemed to hear the words:

> Who, if I cried out, would hear me among the ranks of the angels
>
> *(translated by Martyn Crucefix)*[108]

which became the opening lines of the first of the *Duino Elegies*. It was as if the god of the north wind had touched him.

The French writer Victor Hugo experimented with spiritualism and received some remarkable 'spirit messages' in séances at his home. Such messages are generally the work of elemental beings, according to Steiner. Hugo seemed to encounter an inspiring daimon-like entity calling itself 'Death'. It said:

> During their lives, all great minds create two bodies of work: their work as living beings, and their work as phantoms of the night. Into the living work they throw the living, terrestrial world; into the phantom work they pour that other, celestial world. The living speak to their century in the language that it understands, work with what is possible, affirm the visible, affect the real, light up the day, justify the justifiable, demonstrate proof. Engaged in this work, they fight, they sweat, they bleed; while in this martyrdom genius must bear with imbeciles; a flame it must bear with shadow; the chosen, it must bear with the crowd, and die Christlike, God's dowry to the world, between two thieves, vilely, scorned, and wearing a crown of thorns so heavy a donkey could graze on his forehead . . .
>
> You've been day, come be night; come be shadow; come be darkness; come be the unknown; come be the impossible; come be mystery; come be infinity. You've been the face; come be the skull. You've been the body; come be the soul. You've been the living; come be the phantom. Come die, come be resurrected,

come create, and come be born. I wish that ... Man could
watch you taking flight and confusedly sense your formidable
wings beating in the stormy sky of your Calvary. Living being,
come be wind of night, noise of forest, foam of wave, shadow
of den; come be hurricane, come be the horrible dread of the
savage darkness. If the herdsman shivers, may it be your step
that he has heard; if the sailor trembles, may it be your breath
that he has heard. I bear you away with me; the lightning flash,
our pale horse, rears up in the clouds. Come on! Enough sun.
To the stars! To the stars! ...[109]

It is possible that Hugo was tapping his own subconscious—this is
not meant to be a reductionist statement. Steiner's research revealed
that Hugo had been an initiate of the Hibernian Mysteries, and had
had a special connection to the planetary sphere of Saturn, the
keeper of 'cosmic memory'. Rudolf Steiner describes Hugo as
having much within his soul experience that he could not really
bring out: in the Hibernian mysteries the pupils were led to
experience a great range of soul states, of inner doubt and ques-
tioning, of being led far back into the earth's history and to have
glimpses of the distant future.

> ... what had been retained of the great cosmic retrospect was
> transformed when the soul came down into a physical body
> and underwent a kind of education neither of which in truth
> were suited to experiences lived through in an Hibernian
> Initiation and wrought out in the Saturn sphere. When the soul
> descended, this was all transformed into ideals reaching out to
> the future. But because the body was that of a Frenchman of
> the nineteenth century and therefore altogether different from
> the remarkable bodies of the old Irish initiates, a very great
> deal receded into the background, transforming itself into
> sublime but fantastic pictures, which however have a certain
> power, a certain grandeur about them.[110]

So the thul in some sense visits an inward Thule. Goethe, following his trip to Italy perceived that his creative powers came from
the same source as nature's—the living, weaving etheric, even if he
did not call it by name.

It seems to me that, in creating their works of art, the Greeks proceeded according to nature's own laws, which I am now tracing.[111]

But we must look even beyond a metaphorical Thule. In the human microcosm can we find a region which has a correspondence to the earthly polar or 'hyperborean'? We have already referred to the human head bearing a greater concentration of life ether; let us develop this further. Inside the skull, behind the forehead, lies the pineal gland (epiphysis), atrophied from an earlier organ that in far more distant times served as a kind of sense organ, even causing a projection from the head like a lantern (cf. the etheric 'serpent' in Chapter 6).[112] Around the pineal gland a remarkable activity can take place, allowing light to form. We have discussed the 'unfallen' ether forces of Hyperborea and that the coming of Christ brought them into a human body. These forces are also active in the blood, and when Christ's blood fell to the earth at his crucifixion they began to work at the transformation of the earth so that in the distant future fallen etheric forces can return to an etherized condition. His etherized blood has remained in the earth's ether. Streams of ether move from the human heart to the head as the blood becomes transformed into etheric substance, and if the soul opens to an understanding of Christ these can meet with Christ's etheric streams and unite.[113]

In another lecture, Steiner describes how the pineal gland is nourished by the purest mineral forces and the pure life forces play around it; only the purest sense impressions can reach it. He likens this to the legend of the Holy Grail, which nourishes with the miraculous healing food.[114] Margarethe Kirchner-Bockholt has developed this imagination as of a 'Grail Castle in the Brain', the carbuncle stone which illuminated the castle at night being the pineal gland.[115] Furthermore, Steiner speaks about finding the Grail within as an experience of entering one's innermost heart sanctuary. This can be likened to an inner mystery centre:

In the Temple of the human body is the Holy of Holies. Many people live in the Temple without knowing anything about it. But those who have an inkling of it receive from it the power to purify themselves to such an extent that they can enter into this

holiest place. Therein is the Holy Vessel which has been prepared throughout the ages as a fit container for the blood and
life of Christ when the time for it arrives. When man has
entered therein he has found the way to the Holy of Holies in
the great Temple of the Earth. Therein, too, many are living on
earth without knowing anything about it, but when a person
discovers himself within his innermost sanctuary, he will be
allowed to enter in and there discover the Holy Grail. The
vessel will appear to him as though cut in wonderful shining
crystal which is formed into symbols and letters, until he
gradually senses the sacred contents and it gleams for him in
golden radiance. A person enters the Mystery Centre of his
own heart and a divine being emerges from this place and
unites itself with the God outside, with the Being of Christ. It
lives in the spiritual light which shines into the vessel and
thereby sanctifies it.[116]

Thus in a certain way we can see how the search for an outer
Hyperborea or Thule becomes a search for the Holy Grail after the
time of Christ. For the Grail is about the mystery of Christ's blood,
which having fallen to the earth is then carried in human hearts.
Christ's ego manifests in this blood and together with the unfallen
ethers can thus enter the human being's bloodstream.

Rudolf Steiner further spoke of the Grail in a particular way
when he lectured in Britain in 1924. He contrasted the Grail stream
bearing a more inward form of Christianity, which entered the
blood and the heart, meeting with the pre-Christian Arthurian
stream whose initiates, like those of the northern mysteries,
understood the working of divine beings in nature and the cosmos
(as referred to in connection with the Druids). Following the death
of Christ, these Druid/Arthurian initiates could perceive his Life
Spirit—the completely pure 'body' of life forces—a transformed
ether body, also known as *buddhi* in esoteric teaching. They could
perceive this around the earth. There was an actual meeting of these
two streams, apparently in AD 869, close to the time when the actual
'Parzival' hero—the 'pure fool'—finally entered the Grail Castle
and asked the question 'What ails you?'[117] Students of spiritual
science will recognize the year 869 as being a momentous time in

which, due to machinations of adversary forces, the participants at the eighth Ecumenical Council of Constantinople were 'inspired' by a demonic being to bring about decrees in which the 'spirit' was no longer part of the trinity of body, soul and spirit. Instead the soul was said to have certain spiritual attributes.[118] There was also a heavenly counterpart to this. A little before, roughly during the eighth century, the 'cosmic intelligence' had descended to earth, being granted to human beings to develop. By this is meant an understanding of how cosmic spheres and the beings connected to them interact with one another. It had previously been under the guardianship of the Archangel Michael but now must be allowed to unfold on earth.[119] Initiates knew that when Michael's period of rulership as an archangelic Time Spirit came again in 1879 human beings could look to him in order to spiritualize thinking once more. Moreover this spiritualized thinking must now work to revitalize the earth, in communion with the Christ power.

At Koberwitz in June 1924, Steiner gave the course on bio-dynamic agriculture to enable farmers and gardeners to understand how substances can be used in connection with cosmic forces to nourish the earth. He also gave a lecture to young people during this time, saying at the end:

> To get to know the powers of nature beneath the earth leads to the understanding that the sword of Michael, as it is being forged, must be carried to an altar that lies beneath the earth. There it must be found by receptive souls ... Does the human being today still know what a person had to go through when meeting the birds, what Siegfried had to go through in order to understand the language of the birds? *Wandervogel:*[120] Wotan, Siegfried—this is something that must be felt again, must be understood. One must first find the way from the abstract conception of *Wandervogel* to Wotan, who weaves in wind and clouds and waves of the earth-organism, to the hidden language of the birds, with which one must become acquainted by reviving in oneself the Siegfried-recollection and the Siegfried-sword, which was only the prophetic precursor of the sword of Michael.[121]

This 'sword of Michael' can be seen as the spiritualized thinking power which must come together with the powers of the human heart. Owen Barfield described it thus:

> Steiner found that there has been going forward, throughout history, a real process of withdrawal—excarnation—of the life of the Spirit from its original home in the macrocosm, and thus from the world of nature. Nature, he said, is in fact becoming more and more a mere product, a 'finished work' of the Gods, more and more the lifeless machine, going on by itself, of its own momentum—which the nineteenth century imagined it to be. Nature is really dying! It was in this light that he interpreted that process of contraction of human experience in thinking, from the wide spaces of the universe into its sharp little focus in the brain ... Thus, the Spirit of man, was, for him, really a seed or germ, out of which the dying Spirit of nature seeks to be reborn.[122]

Saving the environment physically, however important, is not enough. We are called upon to be part of the process of re-enlivening a dying earth with our human thinking, feeling and will, which have been awakened to include the spiritual powers. Then not only can Wotan/Odin be met again, but the seeress's prophecy will be fulfilled that Odin's son Vidar will survive Ragnarok, the Twilight of the Gods, defeat the Fenris Wolf:

> Strides forth Vidar   Valfather's son
> The fearless fighter   Fenrir to slay ...
>
> I see green again   with growing things
> The earth arise   from out of the sea;
> Fell torrents flow,   overflies them the eagle,
> On hoar highlands   which hunts for fish.[123]
>
> Lif and Lifthrasir   in the leafage they
>   Will hide of Hoddmimir
> The morning dews   their meat will be
>   They will rear the races of men.[124]

Lif means life, and Lifthrasir equals longing for life. 'In Him was life, and this life was the light of men ...' And a further seeress's prophecy, which could be seen as foretelling the coming of Christ:

A god will come then   an e'en greater one:
I dare not speak   his dreaded name.
Farther forward   few can see now
Than Odin fighting   the Fenris-Wolf.[125]

5. Norway and the Celtic Christian Legacy

In these next chapters we shall be exploring the more specific legacies of the Druids and of the Celtic Church both in the British Isles and Scandinavia before coming to recognize that this legacy combined with the northern mythology no longer belongs exclusively to a specific region or peoples but can be an inspiration for all. We shall begin with an exploration of how the Grail legends became interwoven with Celtic Christianity in Norway.

It was when Rudolf Steiner was lecturing in Oslo (then called Christiania) in 1910[126] that he heard *The Dream Song of Olaf Åsteson* recited at the home of the poet Ingeborg Møller-Lindholm. It had been taken down in the nineteenth century by a minister and folk song collector, Magnus Brostrup Landstad, during the revival of interest in folk tales and songs common to Europe at this time. Steiner applied his methods of spiritual research to it and later on was able to tell the Norwegian members of the Anthroposophical Society more about it. What we have is apparently a fragment of a much longer piece. It describes the experiences of Olaf Åsteson who falls asleep on Christmas Eve and does not awaken until 13 days later on 6 January. During the Holy Nights he goes through an initiation experience. He is led by the light of the moon and passes through the region of the four elements until he comes to the Gjaller Bridge, which in Norse mythology divides Midgard, the earth realm, from Hel, the kingdom of the dead. Here he has to pass three creatures, who represent the unpurified parts of the soul, before reaching the realm of kamaloca or purgatory—Brooksvalin in the song. Two of these are familiar creatures from Norse mythology—the hound Garm and the Midgard Serpent. A bull appears in place of the Fenris Wolf.[127]

> The spirit snake he struck at me
> The spirit hound bit me,
> And lo! The bull did bar the way.
> These are the three beasts of the bridge,
> Most wicked are they all.
>
> The moon shone bright
> And all the paths led far away ...[128]

Having passed over the bridge, he sees the karmic consequence of people's deeds on earth—

I could see a young man
Who in life had killed a child.
Now he must carry him always
And stand in mud to his knee.

In Brooksvalin, where souls
World judgment undergo.

He meets the powers of evil, described as 'Grim Greybeard', whose name implies a distorted view of Odin—one of the names given to Odin was 'Grim', and then he sees how St Michael and his hosts, together with Christ, are victorious over evil and come to weigh the souls—and how those who gave to others and offered help during their life on earth are duly blessed.

The period of the Twelve Holy Nights (or 13, according to how one reckons) is a very special time for the earth. There is a kind of 'gap' between the annual rhythms of the sun and moon, consisting of 12–13 days. Also, following the winter solstice the sun sets a minute or so later each day, but sunrise remains the same for this period. This suggests a pause in the breathing rhythm of the earth and sun, during which certain forces—earth spirits—are able to be very active and awake deep within the earth. It is a time when people in the northern hemisphere traditionally feel dreamier and want to close in on themselves. We celebrate Christmas at a time when pre-Christian people experienced the rebirth of the sun from the depths of the earth. Christmas-Yule has long been a period for merrymaking with family and friends, and the warmth and jollity has a rightful and necessary place in people's lives. However, it is also a time when there is the possibility of reaching a quiet place in the rhythm of life, in which one can enter into stillness and the deeper regions of the soul life. As the plant seeds in the earth's depths are preparing for new growth, so can human souls go through an inner experience in which they penetrate these depths and draw upon certain forces of rebirth if they are in a state of deepened awareness. Whilst in such a state it is possible to become conscious of what human souls would have to undergo if they are alienated from the Christ Spirit and how a catharsis is possible through the power of Christ.[129] Another spiritual event that happens at this time is the possibility of one's astral body having a meeting with one's Life Spirit (a higher part of us which will only be developed properly in a future epoch).

> Upon this meeting with the Life Spirit depends the nearness of Christ Jesus. For Christ Jesus reveals Himself through the Life Spirit. He reveals Himself through a Being of the Realm of the Archangels. He is, of course, an immeasurably higher Being than they ... Thus through this meeting we draw specially near to Christ Jesus at the present stage of development—which has existed since the Mystery of Golgotha—and in a certain respect we may call the meeting with the Life Spirit: the meeting with Christ Jesus in the very depths of our soul.[130]

This is the initiation experience that Olaf Åsteson underwent.

So who was Olaf Åsteson? Was he simply a name in a folk song or did he ever really live? Rudolf Steiner's research revealed some surprising facts which he told to the Norwegian members. He said that the song was much older than people thought, and had originated about AD 400. At that time there was a Christian initiate who founded a mystery school in southern Norway, a Celtic Christian centre inspired by the teachings of St John. 'Olaf' was a mystery name or title, meaning the one who remains after his predecessors and who passes on the blood. 'Åst' means 'love', so he is the 'son of love'. The fragment we know as the *Dream Song* describes his initiation and the complete version would have covered his journey through the entire zodiac.[131] This mystery centre apparently lasted well into the Middle Ages. Unfortunately Steiner never had time to verify this, so can we find any evidence in history?

It is generally supposed that Norway did not become Christian until the end of the tenth and into the eleventh centuries—and then not always willingly. For the background to this we need to look at the fourth century onwards, when the Irish-Celtic Church flourished and began to spread throughout the British Isles, to outlying islands like Orkney and Shetland, and also as far as Iceland. St Patrick, St Columba and St Aidan are famous for their missionary work from centres such as Iona, but there were many lesser known figures who travelled to the rest of Europe. This was a Christianity deriving from the old capacities of the Celtic peoples, many of whom could clairvoyantly perceive the event of Christ's death in the earth's aura. Especially in Ireland the Church was a rich centre of spirituality and learning, the heir to the old Druid mysteries of which we have spoken, in which people could penetrate the secrets of nature and who recognized Christ as 'Lord of the Elements'. We have already indicated something of the sea traffic between Norway, the British Isles and Ireland in these early centuries, so it is quite feasible to imagine Celtic missionaries in Norway earlier than normally accepted.

There are three figures who were prominent in the development of Christianity in Norway, who, though they lived several centuries later than the time indicated, nonetheless hint at a connection with Celtic rather than Roman Christianity, and who could have borne a link with this ancient centre.

St Sunniva

The story is told that Sunniva was the daughter of an Irish king living in the middle of the tenth century. Her father wanted to give her in marriage to a Viking as a tribute, but she refused and left home with a small band of followers in three ships, which were without sails or oars and allowed to drift 'where God pleased'. Two of the ships were carried to Selje island, off the west coast of Norway, and here they formed a spiritual community, Selje Cloister, dwelling in caves in one of which they created a chapel to St Michael. The neighbouring Earl, Haakon, heard of them and was anxious to find them, but they prayed to be left in peace—to die if necessary—rather than be seized by a pagan Viking and his men. Their prayers seemed to be answered when rocks crashed down and blocked the entrances to the caves and Haakon's men could not reach them. It is said that sometime later two men sailing to Trondheim saw a beautiful light shining from Selje. On landing, they discovered a skull, gleaming white and giving off a sweet odour. They journeyed on to meet King Olaf Trygvesson, were baptized as Christians and told him of the find on Selje. Other tales of the mysterious light had also been reported, so the King sailed to Selje and discovered the bodies—Sunniva's in a state of preservation. He built a chapel in her honour, and later a new monastery church was built there named after the English martyr St Alban. Her relics, however, were moved to Bergen in 1170.[132] Dan Lindholm suggests that 'Sunniva' means 'gift of the sun' and that the shining light was there for the Vikings returning to their homeland who may have been seeking for the new light of Christ.[133]

Two King Olafs

King Olaf Trygvesson and the later St Olaf both bear the name 'Olaf'. The story of Olaf Trygvesson certainly seems to have a connection with the Celtic Church. He reigned in Norway from AD 996 to 1000, but before that he had taken part in Viking expeditions, harrying the coasts of Scotland and England. In 994 he was on the Scilly Isles west of the Cornish coast and whilst there heard of a famous seer. He sent one of his men, who pretended to be Olaf himself, to the seer. The seer told the man he was not who he claimed to be, but that he should be faithful to his master, Olaf. Then Olaf himself visited the seer who told him he would become a renowned king and foretold other events which came to pass within the next few days. Olaf was so impressed that he was baptized by the seer, a hermit who was almost certainly a Celtic monk.

The Benedictine abbey on Tresco was not built until the eleventh century, but on the island of St Helen's there was a Celtic chapel dating at least from the eighth century. Some sources say that Olaf was baptized at Andover in Hampshire, but according to the *Anglo-Saxon Chronicle* this was a *confirmation* with King Ethelred as his sponsor—the baptism would of course have already happened. Olaf was chosen as King by the *Althing* (the Parliament) at Trondheim (then called Nidaros) in 996 and tried to introduce Christianity in his country, sadly often by force—which tended to be the normal way in those times.

The later King Olaf Haraldsson, St Olaf, is the one credited with converting Norway, and one legend has it that he was baptized at the age of three by Olaf Trygvesson, suggesting a kind of spiritual lineage. He was caught up in many conflicts and was killed at the Battle of Stikelstad in 1030. At once there were reports of miracles, and he became Norway's patron saint with the cathedral of Nidaros (now Trondheim) built over his grave. Apart from his popularity as a medieval saint, only the name 'Olaf' and that of his mother 'Aasta' (cf. Olaf Åsteson) show any hint that he might have been connected with the mystery stream.[134] Nevertheless it is interesting that we can find a much later memorial to Celtic Christianity at Balestrand on the Sognefjord. Margareth Sophie Green, a vicar's daughter from York, married Knut Kvikne of the Kviknes Hotel, and wanted to build a church for the English visitors who were starting to discover the beauty of the fjords. Sadly she died of tuberculosis in 1894, but in 1897 the little English church in the style of a stave church was built dedicated to St Olaf. The windows commemorate St Olaf, St Columba, St Sunniva and St Margaret. It is still part of the Anglican Communion overseas.

Sone de Nansai and le Grand Saint Graal

The stories and legends surrounding these figures may not be very convincing proof that a Celtic Christian inspired mystery school existed in Norway at this time—especially as some of the converting took place by threat of sword rather than by power of the spirit— but two further tales from sources other than the sagas of the Norse kings show what may be a hidden link. The stories about the Holy Grail are the main source for the continuance of the esoteric Christian stream in the Middle Ages, giving out a teaching veiled in symbol and narrative. These are two lesser known sagas, which seem to have originated in northern France. The Grail stories drew on both Celtic and Middle Eastern sources. The first of these stories, *Sone de Nansai*,[135] tells us of Sone who sails to an island off the coast of Norway where there is a castle founded by Joseph of Arimathaea. Three streams are said to meet there, teeming with fish. The story tells us that Joseph apparently carried to Norway both the Grail Chalice and the Spearhead of Longinus (the centurion who pierced Christ's side). He arrived in Norway and defeated a heathen king and then baptized and married his daughter. He was wounded in the thighs and became known as the Fisher King, founding a community of twelve monks. In this saga many Grail themes are curiously twisted and intertwined, but the story must have circulated in the old Celtic lands for it bears similarities to the story of Bran and the fabulous land of Llychlyn (Lachlan in the Irish-Gaelic) which was a Welsh name for Norway. There is also an echo of it in the Cornish folk song *The Streams of Lovely Nancy* in which three streams meet below a castle of ivory and diamonds on a rocky coastal cliff. Here the symbolic imagery is strangely woven together with what sounds like a more traditional sailor's song:

> On yonder high mountain
> A castle there does stand,
> It is built with ivory
> Near to the black sand.
> It is built up with ivory
> And diamonds so bright,
> It is a pilot for sailors
> In a dark stormy night ...

The second story is from *Le Grand Saint Graal* of Robiers de Borron[136] and tells how in AD 717 in 'White Britain', on Maundy Thursday, Christ appears to a monk who doubts the Trinity and gives him a little book, the *Book of the Holy Grail*. The monk experiences strange elemental powers and angelic visitations. Then on Easter Sunday he finds that the book has vanished. He hears a voice telling him to go and look for it. After Mass he sets out on a journey, for he has been told that he will find a strange beast at a fountain and must follow it to Norway and there find the book. So he comes to the Vale of the Dead and to a crossroads where, under the fountain, he sees the beast. It has a sheep's head, dog's legs, a wolf's body and a lion's tail. Is this not somewhat reminiscent of the Hound, the Serpent and the Bull which confront Olaf Åsteson? The monk's quest eventually leads him to recover the book.

Whether these stories really mean the geographical region of Norway is not so important (not all translations even name it as such, though it is there in the Old French); the use of the name Norway hints at an underlying mystery source of which we have only fragments and glimpses today. In the context of these sagas 'Norway' becomes a kind of code word, a mystery name in itself. The remarkable Norwegian medieval stave churches with their tiered dragon-sporting roofs are an indication that Christianity was founded on an uncommon perception of how the transformation of the earth's forces and a conquering of the 'dragon'—as a symbol of all those forces that would drag us down—must take place. These stave churches have an older relative in the much plainer pre-Conquest wooden church of Greenstead in Essex, England. This seems to point to a hidden thread which surfaces here and there concurrently in Scandinavia and Britain.

The *Dream Song of Olaf Åsteson* does not seem to be found outside of Norway, but some of the soul experiences are described in the Icelandic poem the *Song of the Sun,* sometimes included in the Elder Edda collection, and there is also an echo in the northern English folk song *A Lyke-Wake Dirge.* The *Song of the Sun* is an extraordinary poem describing what appears to be a pre-Christian Northern initiation overlaid with Christian imagery:

> ... For nine days in the Norns' chair
> I sat, then was set on a horse:
> Misshapen suns shone grimly
> Out of the clouds of the air ...
>
> Then I saw there those who had envied
> The fair fortune of others:
> Their breasts were scored with bloody runes,
> Punishing sin with pain ...
>
> Then I saw there those who had taken
> Pity on the sick and poor
> Over their heads the angels read them
> Gospels and sacred psalms ...[137]

A Lyke-Wake Dirge is much shorter and appears to be an account of an after-death experience of the soul. There are, however, some faint echoes of the *Dream Song:*

> This ae nighte, this ae nighte,
> Every nighte and alle
> Fire and fleet and candle-lighte
> And Christ receive thy saule ...
>
> If ever thou gavest hosen and shoon
> Sit thee down and put them on ...
> If hosen and shoon thou ne'er gav'st nane
> The whinnies shall prick thee to the bare bane
> From whinny-muir when thou may'st pass

> To Brig o' Dead thou cam'st at last.
> From Brig o' Dead when thou may'st pass
> To Purgatory fire thou cam'st at last ...

These may or may not derive from the same source as Olaf
Åsteson, but together with the legends and Grail stories they all give
us a tantalizing glimpse of what may once have been a much deeper
mystery teaching that reached from Ireland to Iceland, Norway,
Britain and northern France—the regions where the Celtic and
Germanic peoples met and mingled. They shared a common heritage, an ability to penetrate to the secrets of nature and their myths
and sagas, derived from their mystery centres, have similar features.
These meetings were often fierce and bloodthirsty but behind all the
fighting there appears an attempt by spiritual powers to bring about
a transformation from paganism to Christianity, which could have
grown out of the Druidic mystery tradition. This, however, failed to
blossom owing to forces of hindrance, and so became a hidden
stream. The lectures that Steiner was giving in Oslo offer a clue.[138]
In these, he traces the intentions of the spiritual beings who guide
humanity, inspiring a movement, passing from the Celtic spirituality of earlier times to the Germanic mysteries—whose centres
can still be seen in places such as the Externsteine in Germany—and
thence westwards appearing in the mysteries of the Grail, and so
perhaps allowing a glimpse to emerge of an early Christian mystery
school in Norway.

6. The Number Five and the Etheric Body

In the Grail story of *Parzival* by Wolfram von Eschenbach, we are told that when Parzival had completed his mission and finally asked the question at the Castle of the Grail he could allow himself the longing to return to his wife Condwiramurs. He tells his uncle Trevrizent that he has not seen her for five years. In his book *The Ninth Century*, W.J. Stein comments on this, and that Rudolf Steiner answered his question about it thus:

> Parzival had not seen Condwiramurs for a long time. More than five years had passed since he had seen her. But it is of no consequence how many months or days have passed beyond five years if once the separation has lasted for that period. *The point is the five years,* for, said Dr Steiner, after a five-year separation love is extinguished ... The poet wishes to tell us that when Parzival met Condwiramurs, his connection with her was over and must again be renewed out of the conscious will.[139]

Why *five* years—what can we understand by this? One opinion has been expressed in an earlier publication by a priest of the esoterically-founded church the Christian Community, that ideally there needs to be a five-year period between divorce and remarriage.

> A substantial period is needed to 'unjoin' two people after they have separated ... According to certain esoteric traditions a five-year's interval is thought to be necessary for the etheric bodies to separate and to re-form themselves as single units. After such an interval, the twain, are in actual fact, no longer 'one flesh'.[140]

During marriage (irrespective of legal sanction), the etheric bodies of the couple merge, to give the biblical expression 'one flesh'. This is partly the reason why couples may find it very painful to be apart. The etheric body of male and female are of the opposite sex to the physical—and seek their union also. People rushing into alliances immediately after separating from a partner would do well to consider this. They are carrying into the new relationship some of the etheric forces of the former partner. It is not inconceivable that some of the spectres that inhabit etheric bodies may also take up residence. Second or subsequent unions entered into without a proper period of separation are perhaps more prone to flounder, and this is likely to be one of the reasons why they come apart— though of course there are many other factors. 'Five' seems to be a number connected with marriage and also the wider community (as will become clearer)—5 × 5 for a Silver Wedding anniversary and 10 × 5 for a Golden.

When we pursue the question of the number five itself, we learn that the etheric body itself is fivefold. Viewed supersensibly it reveals a pentagram of flowing currents.

> One is naturally tempted to picture the etheric body in a material way, somewhat like a thin cloud, but in reality the etheric body consists of a number of currents of force. The clairvoyant sees in the etheric body of man certain currents that are exceedingly important. Thus, for example, there is a stream which rises from the left foot to the forehead [see diagram], to a point which lies between the eyes, about half an inch down within the brain; it then returns to the other foot; from there it passes to the hand on the opposite side; from thence through the heart into the other hand, and from there back to its starting-point. In this way it forms a pentagram of currents of force.[141]

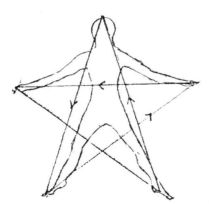

Lines of force in the human etheric body form a pentagram

The directions of these lines of force can be made use of by studying the 'Healing Madonna' series of paintings, mostly by Raphael. They consist of a set of cards that can be purchased and arranged in a particular order in a pentagonal form. Rudolf Steiner indicated that they would thus be beneficial in purifying the astral body and calming disturbances in the soul life.[142]

We now see that 'fiveness' has a special relation to the etheric body, which can in turn affect the astral body, and hence perhaps that this number is involved in the time needed for etheric bodies to be truly free from being closely connected with another. If we consider the important function of the etheric body in sickness and health, it is not surprising that this number five plays a part in healing. Fourfoldness is still connected to the directing power of the gods but with fivefoldness, the possibility of a fifth member, the Spirit Self was granted to humanity. This gift of the future is connected with the whole development of freedom and independence, and from such freedom there is the possibility of doing *evil*.

> No being can do evil who has not arrived at 'fivefoldness'. Wherever we meet with evil, such that it can actually adversely affect our own being, there is a fivefoldness at play.[143]

We can now imagine why a reversed pentagram is connected with black magic and an upright one can be used as a protection against evil spirits.

Because of the beneficial aspect of 'fiveness' and its connection to the etheric body, there is a possibility for healing to make use of 'five' rhythmically—rhythm being one way to understand the workings of the etheric.

> Part of the treatment would be to study the illness in its development on the first and fifth days after its onset, on the separate days at the fifth hour past midnight, and again during the fifth week. Thus it is always the number five that determines when the physician can best intervene.[144]

For the medieval alchemist, 'ether' was the 'quintessence', the fifth essence or energy arising from a combination of the four elements. It is perhaps for the connection of 'five' with evil that the Manichaeans, whose future task will be the transformation of evil, taught of the fivefold light and dark elements—breath of air, wind, light, water, fire, opposed by smoke, fire, darkness, fiery wind, fumes—the five Sons of Man and the five Sons of Satan.[145]

It is our own fifth post-Atlantean epoch that has been given the task of facing and recognizing evil, in preparation for the future transformation.[146] It was perhaps in connection with this that Rudolf Steiner apparently also mentioned a 'fifth chamber of the human heart' that is beginning to evolve.[147]

Returning to the pentagram, an important consideration of it is that it is also a cosmic pattern that appears when the Sun and Venus make a conjunction, i.e. come together, 2 × 5 times during a period of eight years—five 'superior' and five 'inferior' conjunctions (the conjunctions that occur when Venus passes from being evening to morning star and vice versa). It is the 'inferior' conjunctions, i.e. when Venus is between the sun and the earth, that are more significant. These shift their position in relation to the fixed stars and after 1199 years come back to the same places.[148] This pattern marks the beginning of the cultural ages and is not the same as when a new zodiac sign is reached due to the precession of the equinoxes—hence the discrepancies in the dates for the beginning of the Aquarian age. The cultural ages indicate that the consciousness for that particular age is now coming into 'flower'. Thus the cultural ages are dates as follows:

Cancer 7227 BC—first post-Atlantean epoch—ancient Indian
Gemini 5067 BC—second post-Atlantean epoch—ancient Persian
Taurus 2907 BC—third post-Atlantean epoch—Egyptian, Chaldean
Aries 747 BC—fourth post-Atlantean epoch—Graeco-Roman
Pisces AD 1414—fifth post-Atlantean epoch—European
Aquarius AD 3574—sixth post-Atlantean epoch—Slav and eastern European
For a more complete explanation, see Robert Powell, *Hermetic Astrology, Volume 1*.[149]

The connection of this cosmic picture to pentagram forms in the landscape will be followed later. The fact that Venus is involved with a rhythm connected to the etheric body and marriage is more than just a nice association of ideas. Steiner has often referred to the puzzling idea that over the ages the names of Venus and Mercury were reversed.[150] We can best understand how this might have happened in this way: accepting the normal astronomical order of the planets with the sun at the centre, we have: Earth and Moon, Venus, Mercury, Sun, Mars, Jupiter, Saturn + the outer planets. From a geocentric perspective, however, which is the one used in an occult understanding of how souls progress through the planetary spheres after death or in initiation—i.e. with the earth at the centre—we have Earth, Moon, Mercury, Venus, Sun, Mars, Jupiter, Saturn + outer planets. Naturally this is and will be confusing to astrologers who ask if they are supposed to make such a reversal in a horoscope. There is no easy answer and the question cannot be dealt with properly here. On the whole, the traditional usage seems to work—but it is also worth looking at Mercury and Venus as if each contained an element of the other.

The symbol associated with Mercury is the caduceus—the wand of Hermes entwined with two snakes, and it is this connection that we will pursue next. Mercury is also associated with healing and health under the leadership of the Archangel Raphael, and it is the etheric body which is the principal factor in matters of health.

In spiritual science we learn that it is not arbitrary that the serpent carries a connection to the etheric. We have to understand something of evolution from a spiritual perspective. In distant times we learn how the moon separated from the earth and, in so doing, took with it certain forces connected with hardening and with evil. The worst of the forces were removed, leaving behind a kind of water-earth body, and certain harmful forces nevertheless did remain within. The human form was gradually developing and, in doing so, took on the form in its lower regions that we associate with a dragon or serpent:

> But since the worst forces had remained as the ingredients of the water-earth, and since these forces were dreadful elements, man's vapour-portion was drawn ever further down, and out of the earlier plant-form a being gradually evolved that stood at the stage of amphibian. In saga and myth this form, which stood far below later humanity, is described as the dragon, the human amphibian, the lindworm. Man's other part, which was a citizen of the realm of light, is presented as a being which

cannot descend, which fights the lower nature; for example, as Michael, the dragon-slayer, or as St George combating the dragon. Even in the figure of Siegfried with the dragon, although transformed, we have pictures of man's rudiments in their primeval duality. Warmth penetrated into the upper part of the earth, and into the upper part of physical man, and formed something like a fiery dragon. But above rose the ether body, in which the sun's forces were preserved. Thus we have a form that the Old Testament well describes as the tempting serpent, which is also an amphibian.[151]

This should not be imagined as a solid form of today, but something that was beginning to evolve into an amphibian and which had a serpent-like etheric body. The human etheric body in ancient times—particularly those connected to the Atlantean epoch, projected far beyond the physical head.[152] Spirit inspiration saw how it had been endowed with this serpent-like form by luciferic beings, and people with this perception were called 'children of the serpent' or 'serpents' and had the faculty of wisdom—hence the idea that the serpent represents wisdom.[153] The uraeus-serpent in the headdress of the Egyptian pharaohs was a relic of this perception. These visionary initiation powers preceded the deed of Christ. Moses showed his mission to his people by lifting up a serpent,[154] and 'handing over a serpent' was the fourth stage of initiation in the old Norse mysteries in which it was shown that a 'spiritual' backbone had developed also.[155] When Christ sent out his twelve disciples, he said: *'Behold I send you forth as sheep in the midst of wolves: be ye therefore wise as serpents and harmless as doves.'*[156] 'Harmless as doves' should never be forgotten for it means that the poison of the serpent must be transformed. When John the Baptist called the Pharisees a 'generation of vipers' he was not in fact abusing them, but referring to an earlier stage of initiation wisdom. From the time of John's baptisms, those who were more advanced could begin to perceive the etheric body not in a serpent form but as a *lamb*—the newly endowed etheric body was to bear this image of self-offering. The translators of this lecture suggest that the newly evolving human ego was seeking mastery over the physical and that the lamb became a symbol of this identification.[157]

The dragon or serpent has remained an image for the untransformed parts of human nature—in Rudolf Steiner's first mystery play *The Portal of Initiation*, Johannes has a vision of his lower self:

> You guide me back again
> into the spheres of my own being.
> Yet how do I behold myself!
> My human form is lost;
> as raging dragon I must see myself,
> begot of lust and greed.
> I clearly sense
> how an illusion's cloud
> has hid from me till now
> my own appalling form.[158]

Thus, although much wisdom was associated with the image in ancient times, and dragons have been used as noble emblems in various cultures, it bears a dual aspect of being connected to the etheric world but also to the remaining forces of evil within the earth. Though for the Chinese 'dragon currents' relate more to the old Atlantean wisdom knowledge. We have already stated that these forces in Europe and America came to be perceived as something to overcome, and that the stave churches which displayed dragons on the roofs were showing a mastery of these forces, not worship.

In his remarkable book *The Viking Serpent*, Harald Boehlke[159] demonstrates how a pentagram form can be found, building on the Golden Section (see below), which connects the earliest Norwegian settlements that are known today with other points, namely Bergen and Hamar with Mount Store Orkelhø and Blikafjell and Sandsøy just off the coast. Sandsøy—'sand island' is a tiny place where Boehlke found a remarkable cave, Dollstein, containing five grottos. The head of this pentagram points in the direction of the mountain ranges at Store Orkelhø. He considers this pattern was the result of the wisdom knowledge of the Celtic Church which had indeed begun to Christianize Norway earlier than supposed. I greatly appreciate his research and contribution but feel it is not correct to say that the serpent was an object of veneration to those early Christians. After all, St Patrick is said to have banished them

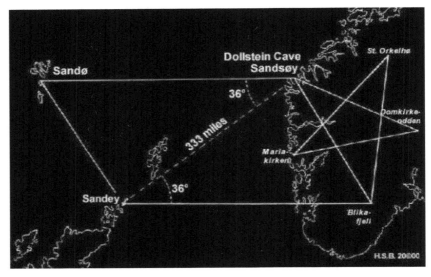

The pentagram and the Sandsøy parallelogram. (Harald Sommerfeldt Boehlke, The Viking Serpent.*)*

from Ireland! Boehlke suggests that serpent veneration stemmed from the 'heretical' Gnostic sect of Ophites who apparently practised serpent handling. This is still done by certain 'charismatic' Christians, especially in parts of the USA. The intention is not to venerate these creatures but to display a mastery over them, an imperviousness to their poison.

In Chapter 1 we learned of the early Druids' experience of earth currents and that these revealed moral qualities to them. We are reminded that these magnetic currents are remains of the Moon stage of earth evolution and are particularly strong where north-south mountain ranges prevail as in America, but also to some extent in Norway.[160] Thus it was perhaps perceived as particularly important to 'tame' these currents in Norway with the healing powers of a pentagram. The knowledge thus possessed by the Celtic Christians would have come to them from the older Druid wisdom. Joseph Schauberg states that in Germany an old name for the pentagram was *Drudenfuss, Druidenfuss* (Druid foot).[161] This was also seen as connected to the pentagonal shape of the feet of the Swan Maidens or Valkyries. It is also noteworthy that the swan was a symbol of the ether body and its organs,[162] an image we looked at in connection with Apollo and Hyperborea. Legends of 'monsters' in lochs and lakes of Scotland, Ireland and Norway—and even alleged sightings today—may well be the remnant of the idea that these currents are still 'submerged' both in the deepest waters, the earth and in our own sheaths. It is worth considering that Rudolf Steiner gave what are sometimes considered his most esoterically Christian lectures, *The Fifth Gospel*, first in Christiania, now Oslo.[163] Joseph Schauberg also suggests that the Gothic style of architecture reached middle Europe from the Celtic Church teachers. The use of the pentagram seems to have been kept somewhat hidden, perhaps because a reversed pentagram was regarded as a symbol of black magic. This was more to do with its 'pagan' use, where it can be seen as reversed on amulets. Much more could be said about the use and symbolism, its appearance in apples and in the rose family. But mention should be briefly made to its relation to the Golden Section or divine proportion, which is well documented, meaning the ratio of the sum of the quantities to the larger quantity is equal to the ratio of the larger quantity to the smaller one— $\frac{1+\sqrt{5}}{2}$ as used in sacred geometry, renaissance art and indeed nature itself.

Connected to the idea of health and healing, the Pythagoreans apparently labelled the five points with the letters U G I EI A—the first letters of Greek words for the elements:[164]

U = Hudor—water
G = Gaia—earth
I = Idea—form/idea, or 'Hieron'—a divine, holy thing
EI = Heile—sun's warmth—heat
A = Aer—air

Thus they could spell out the word *HYGEIA*, meaning health, wholeness and the name of the goddess accordingly. Its connection with cosmology can be seen in the following:

360 ÷ 5 = 72
72° for the angles of the pentagram
1° in 72 years for the precession of the equinoxes
72 or 73 days separates the Sun/Venus conjunctions (both superior and inferior).

72 points in 360° would be 5° apart
72 chapels in the Grail Castle

Why might it be important to know when the Sun/Venus conjunctions occurred? According to Rudolf Steiner, Venus is not only
the bearer of love and beauty but is also the abode of certain luciferic spirits who enter into a kind of opposition or battle with Sun
beings when Sun and Venus come together.[165] This cosmic pattern
repeats itself to give an octagonal form. It is possible that the round
churches of the Templars were based on the octagonal in order to
harmonize this activity. On the island of Bornholm off Denmark
there are a number of round churches, which may or may not be
Templar inspired but whose geometry appears also to be part of the
hidden process of Christianizing Scandinavia and healing the
earth's currents.[166] A combination of pentagonal and octagonal
forms would thus be an important part of esoteric knowledge in
order both to foretell and combat any malign cosmic influences that
might be reflected on the earth, as well as to harmonize those
indwelling in earth currents themselves.

On the cosmic theme, in earlier times the constellations beyond
the zodiac were better known and understood. Serpens—the serpent—writhes above those of Virgo, Libra and Scorpio, all of which
have a bearing on the metabolic organs of the human being. It was
seen as 'held' by Ophiuchus, the Serpent-handler, and connected to
Aesculapius, Greek god of healing, whose feast was celebrated on
the eighth day of the mysteries of Eleusis.[167] This constellation
encroaches on the zodiacal territory between Scorpio and Sagittarius and has given rise to the idea that there are 13 signs of the
zodiac. It is clear from spiritual science that there are only twelve
divine cosmic powers of the zodiac, but this does not mean it has no
significance. It could be seen as a perpetual reminder of the 'lower'
nature or 'dragon' origin of the human form between Sagittarius,
the thighs, Scorpio, the reproductive organs, Libra, the hips and
pelvis, and Virgo, the internal metabolic organs, as from these
regions our human development is constantly under attack,
whether physically, emotionally or morally and has to be held in
check.

It should not be supposed that only America and Scandinavia

The Michael Line—aligned churches and sacred sites dedicated to St Michael

were in need of the harmonizing or controlling of earth energies. In their book *The Sun and the Serpent*[168] Hamish Miller and Paul Broadhurst traced a 'line' from west Cornwall to East Anglia along which are aligned churches dedicated mostly to St Michael, St George or St Margaret, saints all known for their dragon slaying. In addition they have traced winding around this line the 'Michael' and 'Mary' currents across the country and suggest these can be followed across Europe as well. This cross-country 'line' may be because some western parts of the British Isles and Ireland are thought to be remnants from the lost continent of Atlantis, e.g. the legend of the drowned lands of Lyonesse between Cornwall and the Scilly Isles. The large amount of megalithic remains in Cornwall, especially the remarkable number of stone circles in West Penwith alone, suggest the possibility of some form of 'energy', etheric current or 'memory' of Atlantean powers was being guided or 'transmitted' across the region. Is it merely coincidence that Cable and Wireless chose this region to lay their original undersea cable from Porthcurno to America? In these western regions the ancient forces were held in the atmosphere much longer than elsewhere and could be sensed unconsciously.

Other alignments from the sites mentioned in *The Sun and the Serpent* have been traced, but if there are significant pentagram forms between sites in the British Isles they have not so far come to my attention. In southern France, however, in the region around the now well-documented village of Rennes-le-Château, pentagrams formed by natural outcrops and carefully placed buildings have been discovered thanks to surveyors such as Henry Lincoln and David Wood.[169] Suggestions of a sculpted or even 'manipulated' landscape are rife, whether for purposes of initiation or for exercising political 'control' in some form, but these ideas have been and still are being explored by others, and we do not propose to enter these muddier waters here.

Harald Boehlke shows that 'his' pentagram in Norway resembles closely the measurements of ones in the Rennes district.[170] Boehlke discovered a further geometrical pattern that is quite curious, an

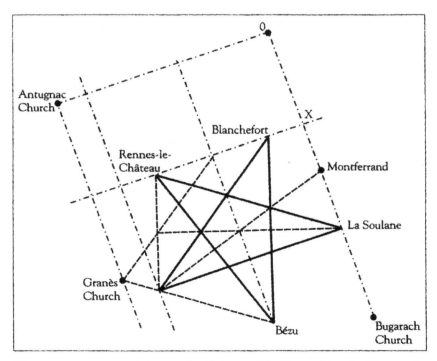

The pentagram around Rennes-le-Château. (© Henry Lincoln, Key to the Sacred Pattern, *Windrush Press 1997.)*

almost perfect parallelogram linking Sandsøy (a western arm of the pentagram) with Sandøy on the Faeroe Islands and Sanday on Orkney—all meaning roughly Sand Island—and Blikafjell. By extending the Sanday (Orkneys)/Blikafjell line he came to a speck of an island in the Baltic, north of Gotland—Gotska Sandøn, the Gothic Sand Island. What could be the significance of these 'sandy' places so linked? Sand has traditionally been a vital ingredient of glass making, containing a high silica content which when heated becomes transparent. It lets in the light. Is this the light of Christ—or another means to combat Lucifer, the Light-bearer? Boehlke had hoped the Norway pentagram would point to Selje cloister, significant in the story of St Sunniva, but instead the arm ends at Sandsøy a little to the north, with its mysterious Dollstein cave about which there is the legend that it continues under the sea to Scotland (a kind of echo of the geometric link with Sanday in the Orkneys?). As an indication of the idea that earth 'dragon' currents must be tamed, there were in Norway in the twelfth century about a thousand churches dedicated to St Michael. In the eighth century there were about six hundred in the British Isles and Ireland, and about seven hundred in France.[171]

The whole theme of earth energies is too vast to be covered here. There are various viewpoints and a considerable literature, but we will make one reference however.

The high quartz content of the stones used for building stone circles and other megalithic sites has often been noted. The light is drawn in and quartz is generally thought to 'hold' etheric energies. In the later 1970s and early 1980s an interesting project called appropriately the 'Dragon Project' was started by Don Robins, Paul Devereux and others to use ultrasonic detectors in and around certain megalithic remains in the British Isles.[172] At sunrise they discovered a strong pulsing close to the Rollright Stones in Oxfordshire, though results were variable. They also experimented with Geiger counters and found in the case of the 'Merry Maidens' circle not far from Penzance in Cornwall that the radiation inside the circle was lower than outside—where, perhaps due to the local granite, it was higher than in other places tested. Unfortunately the experiments—and the book—peter out with the results being inconclusive. That an effect appeared at sunrise matches the diurnal rhythms of the earth's 'breathing', in which a movement of the chemical ether can be seen manifesting physically as dew.[173] Movements of chemical (sound) ether could then be detected by ultrasonic equipment. We have had from Steiner that part of the sound (tone or chemical, number) ether has 'fallen' as it were and formed magnetism, hence making detection with physical instruments possible. Whether 'earth currents' are the same as magnetic currents is unclear and one would not necessarily expect to be able to measure them, especially if they remain at the 'etheric' level. Apart from the astronomical alignment discoveries at megalithic sites by Alexander Thom[174] and others, and summer and winter solstice alignments, research generally is scantier than one would wish. In recent years the Dragon Project has in fact shifted to studying altered states of consciousness, sleep and dream patterns, at ancient sites.

7. The Externsteine and the God Vidar. Finland and Signposts to the Future

We have already mentioned the sacred site of the Externsteine in the Teutoburg Forest in Germany, situated in the area approximately above which Rudolf Steiner suggested 'Asgard' was present spiritually. Its name, as Alfred Heidenreich suggests, may have been contracted from *Sternensteine an der Egge*—Star Stones on the (River) Egge.[175] It is a remarkable site in that it combines traces of pre-Christian worship and ritual with not only medieval Christianity but a medieval element showing an unmistakable esoteric Christian influence.

The four principal huge rocky outcrops have been described and photographed in considerable detail by German researchers such as Hans Gsänger and Rolf Speckner (with particularly striking photographs).[176] At the top of the tallest rock, reached by a bridge from the rock next to it (probably it was once a rope bridge), is a small chamber with a circular window above an altar. Through this the sun rising at the summer solstice could be viewed and the sunset from a window facing it. Lower down, inside the largest rock are three interconnected grottos not normally open to the public where it is thought initiations would have taken place. On the outside is a stone sarcophagus in which someone might have lain for the purposes of initiation. What form might these initiations have taken? In a very early lecture Steiner suggests the following experiences, which he said were taught by the Drotts or Druids, as mentioned earlier. He called it the 'Hunt for Baldur'—meaning the 'unfallen' higher human being which was later revealed by Christ.

First stage: the pupil was led before the 'throne of necessity', to stand in front of the 'abyss', to experience in one's body the plant and mineral kingdoms.
Second stage: experiencing the animal kingdom, passions and desires in oneself as well as penetrating the veil of the senses—an astral world experience, seeing 'the sun at midnight'. **First initiation**.
Third stage: experiencing the elemental powers in the forces of nature.

The Externsteine rocks

Small chamber with stone altar and circular window for viewing sunrise at the summer solstice

Fourth stage: 'Handing over the serpent' by the hierophant. Learning to discern what is true and what is false. The pupil is then endowed with a spiritual backbone after being lifted out of the passions and desires, so that he or she can be raised into the spiralling of the spiritual brain. **Second initiation.**

Gaining access to the labyrinth, which can be likened to the physical convolutions of the brain. **Third initiation.**

Fifth stage: The pupil must take the oath of silence over a naked sword—the secrets must be kept, but sagas could be created so that something eternal might be expressed.

Sixth stage: drinking a draught from a human skull, learning to transcend the human, especially the lower bodily nature.

Seventh stage: The pupil was then shown the path to the higher worlds. The experience he or she had was of a palace with a roof of flashing shields, before he or she became a priest of the sun. This is described in a narrative form in Snorri Sturluson's version of the Edda[177].

Many photos, Rolf Speckner's and others, seem to reveal sculpted figures or faces on the rock surfaces, thought to be the images of gods, but whether these were formed naturally or consciously is uncertain. On many rocks in especially potent landscapes it is not difficult to make out faces or forms, but this is not to say they are all in the eye of the beholder. One of them seems to guard the entrance to the grottos and appears more definitely man-made and is often referred to as St Peter. The lake beside the rocks could also have been used in connection with the Nerthus mysteries for drowning the chariot as Tacitus described.

Not far away it is thought the Irminsul once stood. This was a pillar representing Yggdrasil, thought of as the world axis as well as the Tree of Life, with two branches shaped like ram horns at the top. Irmin or Hermin was another name for the god Heimdall who guarded the Bifrost Bridge leading to Asgard. 'Irmin's Way' was a name for the Milky Way. In England the Great North Road was also called the Milky Way and part of it in Lincolnshire is known as Ermine Street. The Saxon Irminsul, which 'led to the stars', was destroyed by Charlemagne in AD 772.

The medieval carving near the base of the largest rock is a

The Externsteine medieval relief carving showing the deposition of Christ's body from the cross

remarkable example of how pagan beliefs led over to the esoteric Christian and is a kind of representation of a culmination of much we have been discussing. It is thought to date from *c.* 1130. The main part shows the deposition of Christ's body from the cross, carried by Joseph of Arimathaea and Nicodemus. At one side the Irminsul is bowing down before St John holding the Book of

Revelation. At the other side, a Mary, her head broken off, clasps the head of Christ. Above, the Risen Christ holds the oriflamme banner, a flag which was used by Frankish kings. It came to be connected to the Christian mystery school of St Denis or Dionysius the Areopagite, whose teachings originated from St Paul, and bears a Templar-style cross. An oriflamme was also apparently used by the Templars at Gisors. The sun and moon, both veiled, are shown on either side. Under the crucifix are a naked man and a clothed woman caught by a dragon, suggesting Adam and Eve. In Sergei Prokofieff's research, he indicates that Joseph of Arimathaea and Nicodemus in an earlier incarnation had both been pupils of the great initiate Skythianos, of whom we spoke earlier, the initiate who taught the mysteries of the physical body and who guided both the peoples of the Hibernian west and those of the Black Sea region—the Scythians with their leader Sieg (Odin).[178] Therefore these two former pupils were granted the privileged role of handling Christ's body, which in three days would disintegrate and allow the 'phantom' or spiritual essence of the physical to appear in an etheric form at the Resurrection. The physical body when not diseased is the most developed part of the human being, a reminder of the 'image and likeness of God' and of the heavenly zodiac. In the brain is to be found the purest part as we have already discussed, in the 'Grail Castle'. Joseph of Arimathaea, a secret disciple of Jesus Christ and member of the Sanhedrin, received the body in order to bury it in his own tomb and, according to legend, collected the sacred blood in the chalice which was used at the Last Supper, which becomes the Grail vessel. Legends, and the apocryphal Gospel of Nicodemus, state how Joseph was imprisoned for burying Christ's body but the holy chalice nourished him until he was released when Jerusalem was sacked by Vespasian[179] and Titus. Then he travelled to France and on to England, bearing the Holy Blood—the source of the Grail stream—and settled at Glastonbury.

There is a tradition that Nicodemus also collected the Holy Blood and was thus a Grail Bearer too. His connection with the mysteries of the physical body is also shown by the legend in which he was said to have carved a head, a likeness of Christ. A continuation of Chrétien de Troyes' *Perceval* states:

Nicodemus had carved and fashioned a head in the likeness of the Lord on the day that he had seen Him on the cross. But of this I am sure, that the Lord God set His Hand to the shaping of it, as they say; for no man saw one like it nor could it be made by human hands.[180]

He was in fact a Pharisee, a member of the Sanhedrin College of 70, but unlike the rest was far advanced on the path of initiation and visited Christ 'by night', i.e. in the spirit.[181] Christ showed him the new path, how death would pass over into resurrection. Later he defended Christ before the other Pharisees. He was said also to have been the nephew of Gamaliel who tutored St Paul and there is a legend that both Gamaliel and Nicodemus took Stephen's body after his stoning and buried it. Nicodemus was deprived of his office and property and beaten as a result, and died a few days later. His apocryphal gospel describes the trial of Jesus at which he warmly testified, and continues with the episode of Christ's descent into hell.

The Pharisees regarded the physical body as a temple, so we can see how both figures continued to have a connection with the mysteries of the physical body and its future, exemplified by Christ's death and Resurrection.

Visitors to the chapel of Robinson College, Cambridge, may be surprised to see a ceramic copy of the Externsteine carving by John Piper, as it is a sacred site not so well known in Britain.

Vidar

> Will the Wolf swallow   Valfather then;
>   will Vidar avenge him:
> he will sunder   the savage jaws
>   of fearsome Fenrir.[182]

Vidar's name has been linked etymologically to *Widder*, German for ' a ram' (in Old English a 'wether' is a castrated ram). He was a son of Odin and known as 'the silent god'. At Ragnarok the Fenris Wolf, who is one of the three offspring of the adversary Loki, devours Odin, but Vidar, who wears boots made from all the leather pieces left over from shoe-making since the beginning of the world, tears apart the wolf's jaws and thrusts his foot into its mouth, killing it. Thus he overcomes the adversary, avenges his father's death and survives Ragnarok, as the seeress prophesied. The feet, denoted in the zodiac by Pisces, are a symbol of human destiny, towards which our unconscious will bears us. The myth suggests that it is the deeds of human beings which will determine Vidar's having sufficient leather for his boots and overcoming the adversary wolf. In an article by Tom Raines,[183] he considers that when something is unused it retains all its forces, so that we can share the 'spiritual leather', receive a new destiny if we are willing to put on Vidar's boots ourselves.

Thor, Odin's other son, whom we have not mentioned before, was a very popular god with the northern farmers. Inwardly he was really an Archangel like Odin, but remained at the level of the Angel in order to give the Germanic people the ego principle. This works chiefly in human blood (not the bloodstream as in heredity) and Thor's hammer is its pulse beat. The courage of Thor and the other gods was needed to inspire the northern peoples so that this ego principle might develop freely. Working into the blood resulted in the poetic expression of the alliterative verse of Old Norse, the Poetic Edda, and the Old English epic *Beowulf*. It is based on two rhythmic laws—the rhythms of breathing and of blood. A single breath corresponds to four pulse beats (18 and 72 to the minute respectively). This ratio of 1:4 is found in the long line consisting of two half verses separated by a caesura. Each half verse had two strongly accented syllables.[184] (We have tried to maintain these rhythms in the examples quoted in this work.)

Sergei Prokofieff has decribed how Vidar in pre-Christian times was of the rank of an Angel—as a 'son' of Odin—an Archangel, and was in fact the Guardian Angel of the Buddha until he achieved Buddhahood, at which point his Angel was released and could progress to the rank of Archangel. Hence Vidar is the 'youngest' Archangel, but forgoes this rank until 1879 when Michael becomes a member of the Archai.[185] According to this view, it is thus incorrect to state (as has happened in some literature) that Vidar is the same being as Michael. As an Archangel Vidar has a fully developed Life Spirit or Buddhi, and Prokofieff goes on to suggest that his role was to preserve the etheric sheath of the 'Nathan' Jesus child which would have separated from his etheric body at the age of between five to seven, and that he was the same angelic being who assisted Christ in the Garden of Gethsemane. Vidar is thus a 'guardian' of the Nathan soul, and Christ in the etheric world is 'in the garment of the Nathan Soul'. The most important spiritual event of the twentieth century is the reappearance of Christ in the earth's etheric realm—sometimes called the Second Coming, but should never be imagined as another physical incarnation. Vidar fashions the etheric image for Christ, who is surrounded by the light-aura of the Nathan soul as though by a soul sheath. In the myths Vidar was seen as the god who brings rejuvenating forces to humanity and we can thus imagine how, when we are contemplating Christ as the bringer of new tidings and life forces to human beings, we are also united with Vidar.[186] Rudolf Steiner reminded the Norwegian people that nature, too, would receive new life forces if people could only connect with the elemental beings in the light of Christ:

> Gods will reappear as the followers of Christ, as they appeared before the Mystery of Golgotha without Christ. Before the Mystery of Golgotha mankind beheld an ensouled and enspirited Nature. Since the Mystery of Golgotha mankind must strive to see that ensouled and enspirited Nature forms the following of Christ, that the nature spirits are all seen as the followers of Christ, for without Him they cannot be seen. This has been alluded to right here, in the indication to the people here that Vidar will reappear in a new form from out of the hosts of the ancient spirit-beings.[187]

The Fenris Wolf is an ahrimanic entity and is also a symbol of atavistic clairvoyance, which is currently being stimulated as Ahriman wants to create his own kind of occult school. This may account for the many dubious 'visionary' experiences some people of today are having, and which are often atavistic clairvoyant abilities resurfacing. They will allow nature spirits to be perceived in the 'wrong' way and then these beings will fall prey to Ahriman. Vidar's connection with the new twentieth-century ability to see Christ again in the life sphere and the banishing of unhealthy clairvoyance is clearly indicated.

The powers given by the old Archangel Odin, the old clairvoyant powers, cannot save man; something very different must supplant them. These future powers, however, are known to Teutonic mythology; it is fully aware of their existence. It knows that the etheric form exists in which shall be embodied what we are now to see again—Christ in etheric form. He alone will succeed in banishing the dark and impure clairvoyant powers which would confuse mankind if Odin should not succeed in overcoming the Fenris Wolf which symbolizes the atavistic clairvoyance. Vidar who has been silent until now will overcome the Fenris Wolf . . .

Whoever recognizes the significance of Vidar and feels him in his soul, will find that in the twentieth century the power to see the Christ can be given to man again. Vidar who is part of the heritage of Northern and Central Europe will again be visible to man. He was held secret in the Mysteries and occult schools—the god who should await his future mission.[188]

Not only does Vidar protect the newly awakening clairvoyant faculties but we learn that he is also the friend of communal and joint endeavours, such as any groups working from out of an anthroposophical spirit—for as an Archangel he can connect himself with a group of souls.

And if higher spiritual forces are to be awakened in mankind, which we shall certainly see realized in the future, then to use the words of Vidar, the Aesir who has been silent until now, he will become the active friend of co-operative work, of co-operative endeavour, for which purpose we have all assembled here.[189]

So that when considering Vidar, we are leaving the long journey of the past behind and are looking at the present and future and how we can feel the presence of this other spiritual being as our guide and helper.

Greenwoods grow,   and grasses tall,
    in Vidi, Vidar's land:
from horseback leaps   the hero, eager
    to avenge his father's fall.[190]

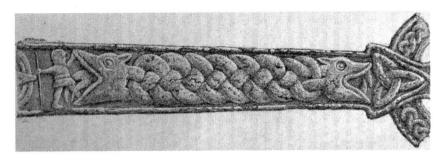

Carving of Vidar overcoming the Fenris Wolf, stone cross (shown on its side) in the churchyard of St Mary's, Gosforth, Cumbria

The Viking cross, Gosforth churchyard

Lest it should be imagined that Vidar somehow belongs only to Scandinavia, we must point out that there are images of him in Britain, dating from the Viking age. The cross in Gosforth churchyard in Cumbria shows him attacking the Fenris Wolf, and an engraved stone found in Scotland at St Andrews and thought to be Pictish shows the figure of a man with a sword tearing apart the jaws of an animal. Odin with a raven is recognizable on horseback with the Fenris Wolf about to swallow him, whilst Vidar stands in the foreground tearing the wolf's jaws apart with a ram (cf. *widder*) standing at the back as Henry Colley March in *Pagan-Christian Overlap in the North* has correctly identified.[191] We should add that it is not simply an image of an animal being destroyed and that real wolves have their place in creation; it is an image that would have been understood as symbolizing an evil being. Therefore, as Christianity was taken from the west eastwards by the early Celtic Church, knowledge of Vidar came back westwards, borne mainly by the newly converted Vikings.

Photo of the Pictish sarcophagus stone at St Andrews, believed to be of Vidar overcoming the Fenris Wolf

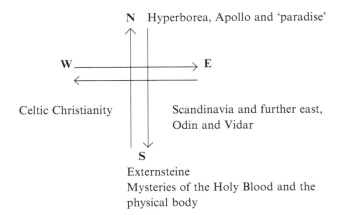

N   Hyperborea, Apollo and 'paradise'

W ——————————————→ E

Celtic Christianity

Scandinavia and further east,
Odin and Vidar

S
Externsteine
Mysteries of the Holy Blood and the
physical body

We can imagine all this in the form of a cross delineating the
movements N—S, S—N and E—W, W—E of these various different streams, through all of which the mystery of Christ's coming
to the earth and his deed for its future transformation were foretold
and can be experienced.

Finland

I have purposely concentrated on the northern European experience. Studies of the entire arctic peoples and global northern regions
would be a vast and fascinating theme but are at present beyond the
scope of this book. However, we can conclude with a brief consideration of that other northern country so close to 'Germanic'
Scandinavia—Finland. Its language belongs to a non-Germanic
language family which includes Estonian, but it shares many historical and cultural features with its Scandinavian neighbours—the
inhabitants are not mainly Slavs—and it also has a painful history
of trying to break free of Russian domination. In the struggles with
Russia it was the antichristian retarding Bolshevik forces that tried
to dominate the Finns. Even its geographical position placed
between Scandinavia and Russia suggests it has a task more connected to the future—the next or sixth cultural epoch sometimes
called the Russian or Slavic. In the north of Finland are found the
Sami people in Lapland (which extends into northern Scandinavia),
a close-knit people who try to maintain traditional lifestyles, dis-

tinctive colourful clothing and reindeer herding. Though mainly
Christian today, their older beliefs centred on strong magical
shamanic practices and they were viewed in Viking times as *the*
peoples who could practise or teach magic. Into modern times
stories are told of their powers of healing by song and speech, which
draw on the sounds of nature, harmonies detected in trees, mountains, lakes and animals. Curiously the Estonian island of Saaremaa
has also been a contestant for Thule, with the idea that 'Thule' is
derived from the Finnish word *tule*, 'of fire', the Kaali meteor crater
on Saaremaa being the place where the 'sun went to rest'.[192]

The region of Finland was also part of that area which in earlier
times was guided by the initiate Skythianos. His purpose was also to
be able to reach the inner depths of human souls so that they might
be ready to receive the Mystery of Golgotha. But in earlier times he
was also the inspirer of song, rhythmic speech and music played on
early instruments, possibly a kind of pan-pipes, the remnants of
such powers were practised by the bards and skalds in the west and
north and are found in the stories of Apollo and Orpheus among the
Greeks. We find thus another example of the creative power of the
sound-ether. But already by the time folk myths were being passed
on the Finnish people had an inkling of the idea of a threefoldness
of the soul. This threefoldness is often described by Rudolf Steiner
as being as follows: the sentient soul, which is connected more to the
impulses of will, the passions and reactions; the intellectual or mind
soul, which has learned to analyse and control reactions; and the
consciousness or 'spiritual' soul, in which the human ego comes best
to expression. In the present epoch we have reached the age of the
consciousness soul with its clarity and detachment, though not all
people are yet fully at this stage. This threefoldness was expressed in
the great national epic the *Kalevala*, as the three characters
Väinämöinen (sentient soul), Ilmarinen (intellectual soul) and
Lemminkäinen (consciousness soul).[193] Ilmarinen, the master
smith, forges the Sampo—a mysterious vessel that represents the
human etheric body—from the supersensible world of clairvoyance.
The etheric body later lit up as the intellectual soul. In a sense
people learned to bring forth the hidden Sampo and the epic tells of
its theft, loss and re-forging. Steiner speaks about the *Kalevala*
becoming the 'conscience' of Europe in that its forces are not just of

the past but are alive and can work on into the future. In the *Kalevala*, the term 'rune' is used to denote a verse or series of verses; not a single letter, but its etymological origin is the same. Poems were often chanted rhythmically by two people seated facing one another who swayed backwards and forwards—an echo of the former sense for the sound-ether qualities. The final poem is the story of the virgin Marjatta—so virginal that she will not even eat the meat from an animal that has mated—who is mysteriously impregnated by consuming a whortleberry and gives birth to a special child who is baptized and is reared to become a king of the Karelia region. Rudolf Steiner speaks of this as follows:

> I would like to say that, for my feeling, there is altogether no portrayal of Christianity to be found anywhere as delicate and wonderfully impersonal as that found at the end of the *Kalevala*. The Christian principle is freed from any geographic limitations ... At the end of the *Kalevala* we find the penetration of the noblest cultural pearl of humanity into the Finnish culture delicately hinted at as the most intimate concern of the heart of humankind ... In the moment when Christianity enters in, Marjatta's son is baptized, Väinämöinen departs from his people in order to go to an undetermined destination. He leaves his folk with only the content and power of what he, through his singing, had been able to tell them concerning the ancient mysteries included in the history of this people ... Something has happened that brings together this particular folk with the universal human. Here at this point in one of the greatest, most significant and meaningful national epics, where the story leads into an entirely impersonal and— please pardon the paradoxical expression—non-Palestinian description of the Christ impulse, the *Kalevala* leads us to feel the happiness and beneficence manifested by the Sampo when it continues working through all human evolution, when it is experienced working together with the Christian idea, with the Christian impulse.[194]

He thus felt the powers of the *Kalevala* epic as having something to give to the whole of humanity. The poems, collected in the nineteenth century by Elias Lönnrot, are rightly honoured by the

Finnish people and have inspired artists such as the composer Sibelius.

In the stories, part of the struggles are with the people of 'North Farm' or *Pohjola*, imagined as a prosperous Viking-style farm but one that is also cold and gloomy and near to Death's domain. Some writers suppose it to refer to the Lapland region; however it is more the case of representing hardening, adversarial powers that are nonetheless necessary for evolution. So in Finland further north was not imagined as paradisaical but potentially dark and harmful. The discriminatory powers of the Finns could perceive a shadow side to the north, which we touched on earlier. This could be connected to the nature of the future sixth epoch, which will in a certain sense mirror the second, the 'Persian' epoch when the initiate Zarathustra taught of the battle between light and dark. In the sixth epoch the Manichaean stream will bear fruit, having developed the ability to begin to absorb the dark in order to convey it back to the light, not merely to understand evil—the task of the fifth epoch—but to transform it. Light-filled Marjatta (she calls upon the sun for help) has to stand up to powers threatening her child, but somehow their threats are overcome, she is not turned out of the community as a single mother, goodness prevails.

Thus we end with a northern people who could tell of Christianity in their own way, which points to a future time when Vidar is also recognized and the northern 'magic' is not a fearful demonic kind but a Christ-light-filled one, when new clairvoyant faculties will be within the reach of all humanity. For this, the figure of the initiate Skythianos, unknown to outer history, at different periods prepared groups of souls from the Hibernian mystery regions of the west, to the Scythians of the Black Sea region and to peoples extending throughout Europe to the far north and into Russia, where the next chapter of evolving humanity is to unfold.

Epilogue: A Sea Crossing

There in the ship, the white monk spoke
  And I knew it was true, as the prow cleaved the sea
    Spray sparkling silver on my face
      And the knowing of the mist on the low island hills.
Knew it was true yet must still heed
  Odin and steer by Tyr's star.
'The dragon is conquered' he said,
  'You must put dragons on the roofs, not the prows of your
    ships,
    Your ship is your temple now,' he said.
But I had to face Odin still
  And Freya was my hope after death, not
    Hel's fearful cave.
'Your god Vidar is his servant,' he said,
  But I wasn't convinced.
    'Vidar is silent,' I said, 'He won't tell us till Ragnarok'
'That's happened, it's over,' said the monk,
  'We have the new land, the greening,
    The first man and the woman reborn.'

'We must cast staves, ask the Norns, I want to believe.'
  But the sun had just set and the monk fell asleep,
    A light on his head that I couldn't explain.
I had then to haul in the sail as the sea rose much higher
  The wind full of Odin's wild hunt.
'I want to believe, to believe,' I said as the
  Waves washed over the ship and the hull
    Groaned in the terrible jaws of Thor's fiendish snake.
'I want to believe it is conquered and
  Wolf Fenrir has lost all his power.'
As Ran's rage grew greater, the ship split apart
  And I saw a white pathway through the huge swell,
    And the monk took my hand—
The sun must have risen, for nothing could I see for the
  glory . . .

Notes

RSP = Rudolf Steiner Press
AP = Anthroposophic Press
TL = Temple Lodge Publsihing

Introduction
1. Peter Davidson, *The Idea of North*. London: Reaktion [*sic*] Books Ltd 2005.

Chapter 1
2. William Morris, *Iceland First Seen*, from *Poems By the Way*, 1891.
3. Rudolf Steiner, *Cosmic Memory*, GA 11, Blauvelt: Garber Communications Inc. 1990.
4. For a summary of cymatics as it is often called, see www.cymascope.com/cyma_research/history.html and Masaru Emoto, *The True Power of Water*, Oregon: Beyond Words Publishing Inc. 2003.
5. Aubrey T. Westlake, *The Pattern of Health*, Shaftesbury: Element Books 1985.
6. Ernst Lehrs, *Man or Matter*, Chapter XIX, London: RSP 1985. Rudolf Steiner, Basel 1 October 1911, 'The Etherisation of the Blood', in *Esoteric Christianity*, GA 130, London: Rudolf Steiner Press 2000.
7. Hans Mändl, *Vom Geist des Nordens,* Stuttgart: Mellinger Verlag 1966.
8. London: Anthroposophical Publishing Co. 1932.
9. Rudolf Steiner, lecture, Dornach 13 October 1923, GA 351, 'Man in the Earth in Northern and Southern Regions', Typescript Z 300.
10. J.W. von Goethe, *Scientific Studies*, New York: Suhrkamp Publishing Inc. 1988.
11. Rudolf Steiner, lecture, Dornach 8 December 1923, GA 232, in *Mystery Knowledge and Mystery Centres,* London: RSP 1997.
12. Richard Seddon, *The Mystery of Arthur at Tintagel*, London: RSP 1990.
13. Rudolf Steiner, lecture, Berlin 3 May 1909, GA 107, in *The Being of Man and His Future Evolution*, London: RSP 1981.
14. Rudolf Steiner, lecture, Berlin 25 October 1905, GA 93a, in *The Foundations of Esotericism*, London: RSP 1983.

15. Rudolf Steiner, lecture, Landin 29 July 1906, GA 97, in *The Christian Mystery*, Gympie: Completion Press 2000.
    Basel 20 September 1909, GA 114, in *The Gospel of St Luke/ According to Luke*, London: RSP 1988/Great Barrington MA:AP 2001.
16. Sergei O. Prokofieff, *The Spiritual Origins of Eastern Europe and the Future Mysteries of the Holy Grail*, London: TL 1993.
17. Rudolf Steiner, lectures Vienna 21–31 March 1910, GA 119, *Macrocosm and Microcosm*, London: RSP 1968.
18. Rudolf Steiner, lecture Berlin 23 March 1906, GA 54, not translated.
19. See note 15.
20. See note 16.
21. Rudolf Steiner, lecture Stuttgart 13 August 1908, GA 105, in *Universe, Earth and Man*, London: RSP 1968.
22. For a fuller explanation of the post-Atlantean epochs see Chapter 6.
23. Rudolf Steiner, lecture Berlin 21 October 1904, GA 92, 'Greek and Germanic Mythology', Typescript Z 331.
24. Rudolf Steiner, lecture Stuttgart 14 August 1908, GA 105, in *Universe, Earth and Man*.
25. See Chapter 7.
26. See for instance, Simon James, *The Atlantic Celts. Ancient People or Modern Invention?* London: British Museum Press 1999.
27. Jürgen Spanuth, *Atlantis of the North*, London: Sidgwick and Jackson 1976.
28. Dudley Wright, *Druidism, the Ancient Faith of Britain.* London: Ed. J. Burrow & Co. Ltd. 1924.
29. Frank Teichman, 'The Druid Stone Sketch and St John's Tide Imagination', in *Anthroposophy Today* No. 7 Summer 1989.
30. Rudolf Steiner, lecture Dornach 9 September 1923 (GA unknown), 'Oral Description of the 1923 Visit to Britain', see *Rudolf Steiner Speaks to the British*, London: RSP 1998.
31. Ibid.
32. Rudolf Steiner, lecture, St Gallen 16 November 1917, GA 178, 'The Mystery of the Double. Geographic Medicine', in *Secret Brotherhoods*, Forest Row: RSP 2004.
33. *The Vinland Sagas. The Norse Discovery of America*, London: Penguin Books 1965.
34. Andrew Sinclair, *The Sword and the Grail*, London: Century 1993.
35. Vilhjalmur Stefansson, *Ultima Thule. Further Mysteries of the Arctic*, London: Harrap 1942.

36. See for instance in Eleanor Merry, *The Flaming Door*, East Grinstead: New Knowledge Books 1962.
37. Hamish Miller and Paul Broadhurst, *The Sun and the Serpent*, Launceston: Pendragon Press 1989.
38. Geoffrey of Monmouth, *The History of the Kings of Britain*, London: Penguin Books 1966.
39. Donald Attwater, *The Penguin Dictionary of Saints*, London: Penguin Books 1965.

Chapter 2

40. Jocelyn Godwin, *Arktos. The Polar Myth in Science, Symbolism and Nazi Survival*, London: Thames and Hudson 1993.
41. Ortrud Stumpfe, *Absturz in den Selbstverrat*, Stuttgart: Mellinger Verlag 1993.
42. Rudolf Steiner, lecture Christiania (Oslo) 17 June 1910, GA 121, in *The Mission of the Individual Folk Souls*, London: RSP 1970.
43. Quoted in Spanuth, see note 27.
44. Pindar, *Pythian X*, translated by Dawson Turner, London 1852.
45. Pausanias, *Attica* 31.
46. See note 27.
47. Strabo, *Geography* II: 6. 1–2, Loeb Classical Library Vol. V, p. 245.
48. See note 27.
49. Strabo, *Geography* IV. Loeb Classical Library Vol. II.
50. William of Malmesbury, *The Kings Before the Norman Conquest*, facsimile reprint, Llanerch Enterprises 1989.
51. Sigrid Undset, *Happy Times in Norway*, London: Cassell and Co. 1943.
52. *American Journal of Philology*, Vol. 103, 1982.
53. Rudolf Steiner, lecture, Dornach 23 July 1922, GA 214, in *The Mystery of the Trinity*, Hudson: AP 1991.
54. Rudolf Steiner, lecture, Stuttgart 13 August 1908, GA 105, in *Universe, Earth and Man*, London: RSP 1987.
55. Rudolf Steiner, lecture, Dornach 2 October 1916, GA 171, in *The Knights Templar*, Forest Row: RSP 2007.
56. Snorri Sturluson, *Edda*, translated by Anthony Faulkes, London: Dent 1987.
57. Tacitus, *Germania (Agricola and Germania)*, London: Penguin Books 2010.
58. Rudolf Steiner, lecture, Basel 21 December 1916, GA 173, in *The Festivals and Their Meaning*, London: RSP 1996.

59. See note 27.
60. See note 58 and Bruce Dickins, ed. *Runic and Heroic Poems of the Old Teutonic Peoples*, New York: Kraus Reprint Co. 1968.
61. Rudolf Steiner, lecture, Leipzig 30 December 1913, GA 149, in *Christ and the Spiritual World*, London: RSP 1963.
62. Rudolf Steiner, lectures, Basel 15–26 September 1909, GA 114, *The Gospel of St Luke/According to Luke*, London: RSP 1988/Great Barrington MA: AP 2001.
63. See note 58.
64. Rudolf Steiner, lecture, Torquay 18 August 1924, GA 243, in *True and False Paths in Spiritual Investigation*, London: RSP 1969.
65. See note 62, especially Lecture Seven.
66. Rudolf Steiner, lecture, Copenhagen 8 June 1911, GA 15, in *The Spiritual Guidance of the Individual and Humanity*, Hudson: AP 1992.

Chapter 3
67. See note 7, and Chapter 6.
68. Hans Heinrich Engel, *The Mythology of Language*, in Karl König, ed. *On Reading and Writing*, Camphill Books 2002.
69. 'Sayings of the High One', from *The Poetic Edda*, translated by Lee M. Hollander, Austin: University of Texas Press 1990.
70. See note 57.
71. 'The Sayings of Har', from *The Poetic Edda*, see note 69.
72. Rudolf Steiner, lecture, Helsinki 13 April 1912, GA 136, in *Spiritual Beings in the Heavenly Bodies and in the Kingdoms of Nature*, Hudson: AP 1992.
73. See note 21.
74. Jakob Streit, *Sun and Cross*, Chapter 6, Edinburgh: Floris Books 2004.
75. Rudolf Steiner, lecture, Christiania (Oslo) 14 June 1910, GA 121, in *The Mission of the Individual Folk Souls*, London: RSP 1970.
76. Rudolf Steiner, lecture, Neuchâtel 18 December 1912, GA 130, in *Esoteric Christianity*, London: RSP 2000.
77. 'The Lay of Fafnir', from *The Poetic Edda*, see note 69.
78. 'The Lay of Sigdrifa', ibid.
79. Rudolf Steiner, lecture, Berlin 21 October 1904, GA 92, 'The Siegfried Saga', Typescript Z 331.
80. Rudolf Steiner, lecture, Torquay 18 August 1924, GA 243, in *True and False Paths in Spiritual Investigation*, London: RSP 1969.
81. 'All-Wise's Sayings', in *The Poetic Edda*, translated by Carolyne Larrington, Oxford University Press 1999.

82. Louis J. Rodrigues, *Anglo-Saxon Verse Charms, Maxims and Heroic Legends*, Pinner: Anglo-Saxon Books 1994.
83. Rudolf Steiner, lecture, Dornach 10 September 1923, GA 228, 'The Sun-Initiation of the Druid Priest', see *Man in the Past, the Present and the Future*, London: RSP 1982.
84. Snorri Sturluson, *Edda*, London: J.M. Dent 1992.
85. Snorri Sturluson, 'The Ynglinga Saga' in *Heimskringla*, London: J.M. Dent 1930.
86. Tamara Talbot Rice, *The Scythians*, London: Thames and Hudson 1961.
87. London: Penguin Books 1966.
88. London: Everyman, Dent 1992.
89. George Vernadsky, *The Origins of Russia. The Ancient Slavs and the World of the Steppes*. Oxford: Clarendon Press 1959.
90. London: Macmillan 1879.
91. Rudolf Steiner, lecture, Dornach 8 November 1916, GA 292, 'The History of Art', Typescript R 11.
92. London: Faber 1961.
93. Jacqueline Memory Paterson, *Tree Wisdom*, London: Thorsons 1996.
94. Adrian Anderson, *Living a Spiritual Year*, p. 204, Hudson: AP 1993.
95. Ernst Uehli, *Nordisch-Germanische Mythologie*, Stuttgart: Mellinger Verlag 1984.
96. Rudolf Steiner, lecture, Christiania (Oslo) 12 June (evening) 1910, GA 121, in *The Mission of the Individual Folk Souls*, London: RSP 1970.

Chapter 4

97. See note 40. Nicholas Goodrich-Clark, *The Occult Roots of Nazism*, Aquarian Press 1985.
98. Vilhjamur Stefansson, *Ultima Thule*, London: Harrap 1942.
99. Ibid.
100. *Beowulf*, text and translation by John Porter, Hockwold cum Wilton: Anglo-Saxon Books 1995.
101. Nigel Pennick, *Rune Magic*, Thorsons, Aquarian Press 1992.
102. 'The Sayings of Har', vv. 111 and 113, in *The Poetic Edda*, translated by Lee M. Hollander, Austin: University of Texas Press 1990.
103. 'The Lay of Vafthrudnir', vv. 8–9, ibid.

104. *Beowulf*, translated by Seamus Heaney, London: Faber and Faber 1999.
105. *The Vinland Sagas*, London: Penguin Books 1965.
106. Stephen Coote, *John Keats. A Life*. London: Hodder & Stoughton 1995.
107. John Keats, *Poetical Works*, Oxford University Press 1937.
108. Rainer Maria Rilke, *Duino Elegies*, translated by Martyn Crucefix, London: Enitharmon Press 2006.
109. John Chambers, *Victor Hugo's Conversations with the Spirit World*, Rochester, Vermont: Destiny Books 2008.
110. Rudolf Steiner, lecture, Breslau 10 June 1924, GA 239, in *Karmic Relationships*, Vol. VII, London: RSP 1973.
111. Rudolf Steiner, quoted in lecture, Dornach 3 June 1923, GA 276, in *The Arts and Their Mission*, Spring Valley: AP 1964.
112. Rudolf Steiner, lecture, Stuttgart 11 August 1908, GA 105, in *Universe, Earth and Man*, London: RSP 1987.
113. Rudolf Steiner, lecture, Basel 1 October 1911, GA 130, 'The Etherization of the Blood', in *Esoteric Christianity*, London: RSP 2000.
114. Rudolf Steiner, lecture, The Hague 25 March 1913, GA 145, in *The Effects of Esoteric Development*, Hudson: AP 1997.
115. *The Golden Blade* no. 27, 1975.
116. Rudolf Steiner, undated esoteric lesson in *Concerning the History and Content of the Higher Degrees of the Esoteric School 1904–1914/ Freemasonry and Ritual Work*, GA 265, Isle of Mull: Etheric Dimensions Press 2005/Great Barrington MA: SB 2007.
117. Rudolf Steiner, lecture, Torquay 21 August 1924 and London 27 August 1924, GA 240, in *Karmic Relationships* Vol. VIII, London: RSP 1975.
118. Ibid. 27 August 1924.
119. Rudolf Steiner, lecture, Arnhem 19 July 1924, GA 240, in *Karmic Relationships* Vol. VI, London: RSP 1989.
120. Lit. 'Wandering bird'—German youth movement of the early twentieth century.
121. Rudolf Steiner, lecture, Koberwitz 17 June 1924, GA 217a, *Youth's Search in Nature*, Spring Valley: Mercury Press 1979.
122. Owen Barfield, 'Man, Thought and Nature' in *Romanticism Comes of Age*, London: RSP 1966.
123. 'The Prophecy of the Seeress', vv. 53 and 58, in *The Poetic Edda*, translated by Lee M. Hollander.

124. 'The Lay of Vafthrudnir', v. 45, ibid.
125. 'The Short Seeress' Prophecy', v. 17, ibid.

Chapter 5
126. Rudolf Steiner, lectures, Christiania (Oslo) 7–17 June 1910, GA 121, *The Mission of the Individual Folk Souls*, London: RSP 1970.
127. In Norse mythology Garm was a fierce dog guarding the Gjaller Bridge, who fought the god Tyr, causing the death of both. The Midgard Serpent wrapped itself around the earth and was killed by Thor, who died from its poisonous breath. The Fenris Wolf was the offspring of Loki, the adversary god and the giantess Angrboda. At the Twilight of the Gods (Ragnarok) it killed Odin and was in turn killed by his son Vidar.
128. Rudolf Steiner, lecture, Dornach 31 December 1914, GA 275, in *Art as Seen in the Light of Mystery Wisdom*, translated by Pauline Wehrle, London: RSP 1996.
129. Rudolf Steiner, lecture, Hannover 26 December 1911, GA 127, in *The Festivals and Their Meaning*, London: RSP 1996.
130. Rudolf Steiner, lecture, Berlin 20 February 1917, GA 175, in *Cosmic and Human Metamorphoses*, Blauvelt NY: Garber Communications Inc. 1989.
131. See note 128.
132. Sigrid Undset, *Saga of the Saints*, Sheed and Ward 1934.
133. Dan Lindholm, *Stave Churches in Norway*, London: RSP 1969.
134. Snorri Sturluson, *Heimskringla (The Norse Kings Sagas)*, Part One, 'The Olaf Sagas', London: J.M. Dent 1970.
135. *Sone de Nansai*, ed. M. Goldschmidt, Tübingen, 1899.
136. *Le Grand Saint Graal or the History of the Holy Grail*, translated by Henry Lonelich, AD 1450, from the French Prose 1150–1200 of Sires Robiers de Borron; ed. F.J. Furnivall, Early English Text Society, 1874.
137. *The Song of the Sun*, from *Norse Poems*, translated by W.H. Auden and Paul B. Taylor, London: Faber 1983.
138. See note 126, especially lecture 7 of 12 June 1910.

Chapter 6
139. W.J. Stein, *The Ninth Century*, 'Adventure XVI', London: TL 1991.
140. *Marriage*, The Christian Community Press, n.d., out of print .
141. Rudolf Steiner, lecture, Basel 17 November 1907, GA 100, in 'Notes on St John's Gospel', Typescript EN 50.

142. See Brian Gray, *Discovering the Zodiac*, in the 'Raphael Madonna Series Arranged by Rudolf Steiner', *Journal for Star Wisdom*, 2013. Sets of cards can be purchased from Wynstones Press— www.wynstonespress.com

143. Rudolf Steiner, lecture, Stuttgart 15 September 1907, GA 101, in *Occult Signs and Symbols*, New York: AP 1972.

144. Ibid.

145. Richard Seddon, *Mani. His Life and Work Transforming Evil.* London: TL 1998.

146. Rudolf Steiner, lecture, Dornach 25 October 1918, GA 185, in *From Symptom to Reality in Modern History*, London: RSP 1976.

147. This mysterious statement appears to occur only according to Ehrenfried Pfeiffer in his *Heart Lectures*, no. 1, 17 December 1950, Spring Valley: Mercury Press 1982.

148. Joachim Schultz, *Movement and Rhythms of the Stars*, Edinburgh: Floris Books 1986.

149. Sophia Perennis, 2006.

150. See for instance lecture, Düsseldorf 15 April 1909 evening, GA 110, in *The Spiritual Hierarchies and the Physical World*, Hudson: AP 1996. This edition also contains a helpful explanation of the mystery by Georg Unger.

151. Rudolf Steiner, lecture, Leipzig 7 September 1908, GA 106, in *Egyptian Myths and Mysteries*, Spring Valley: AP 1971.

152. Rudolf Steiner, lecture, Stuttgart 4 August 1908, GA 105, in *Universe, Earth and Man*, London: RSP 1987.

153. Rudolf Steiner, lecture, Berlin 23 November 1909, GA 117, in *Deeper Secrets in Human History*, London: Anthroposophical Publishing Co. 1957.

154. Rudolf Steiner, lecture, Hamburg 25 May 1908, GA 103, in *The Gospel of St John*, New York: AP 1984.

155. Rudolf Steiner, lecture, Berlin 30 September 1904, GA 93, in *The Temple Legend and the Golden Legend*, London: RSP 1997, see also Chapter 7.

156. Matthew 10:16.

157. See note 153.

158. Rudolf Steiner, *The Portal of Initiation [Four Mystery Dramas]*, Scene 2, GA 14, London: RSP 1997.

159. Harald Sommerfeldt Boehlke, *The Viking Serpent*, Victoria BC: Trafford Publishing 2007.

160. See note 32.

161. Joseph Schauberg, *Symbolik der Freimauerei, Bd. I, Kapitel XXVII*, Schauffhausen 1861.
162. Rudolf Steiner, lecture, Berlin 6 May 1909, GA 57, 'European Mysteries and their Initiates', in *Anthroposophy*, Vol. 4 No. 3 Michaelmas 1929.
163. Rudolf Steiner, lectures, Christiania (Oslo), Berlin and Cologne, 1913–1914, GA 148, *The Fifth Gospel*, London: RSP 1995.
164. Priya Hemingway, *The Secret Code*, Evergreen 2008.
165. Rudolf Steiner, lecture, Dornach 23 December 1923, GA 232 in *Mystery Knowledge and Mystery Centres*, London: RSP 1997.
166. Erling Haagensen & Henry Lincoln, *The Templars' Secret Island*, London: The Windrush Press 2000.
167. Albert Pike, *Morals and Dogma of the Ancient & Accepted Scottish Rite of Freemasonry*, 1871, or www.forgottenbooks.org
168. Hamish Miller & Paul Broadhurst, *The Sun and the Serpent*, Launceston: Pendragon Press 1990.
169. Henry Lincoln, *The Holy Place*, London: Jonathan Cape 1991. David Wood, *Genisis [sic]*, Tunbridge Wells: The Baton Press 1985.
170. See note 159.
171. Achim Hellmich, 'Der Lichtweg von aussen nach innen', in *Das Goetheanum* 2002, Nr. 40.
172. Don Robins, *Circles of Silence*, London: Souvenir Press 1985.
173. Guenther Wachsmuth, *The Etheric Formative Forces in Cosmos, Earth and Man*, London: Anthroposophical Publishing Co. 1932.
174. Alexander Thom, *Megalithic Lunar Observatories*, Oxford University Press 1973.

Chapter 7
175. Writing in a Christian Community Journal, no date available.
176. Hans Gsänger, *Die Externsteine*, Schaffhausen: Novalis Verlag 1985. Rolf Speckner & Christian Stamm, *Das Geheimnis der Externsteine. Bilder einer Mysterienstätte*, Stuttgart: Urachhaus 2002.
177. See note 155.
178. Sergei O. Prokofieff, *The Spiritual Origins of Eastern Europe and the Future Mysteries of the Holy Grail*, Part 1, Chapter 3, London: TL 1993.
179. *The Apocryphal New Testament*, translated by Montague Rhodes James, Oxford: Clarendon Press 1972.
180. From www.veling.nl/anne/templars/mysteries.html.
181. John 7:50–1.

182. 'The Lay of Vafthrudnir', v. 53, in *The Poetic Edda*, translated by Lee M. Hollander, Austin: University of Texas Press 1990.

183. 'Vidar's Boot, a Glimpse into Our Past, Present and Future', in *New View*, no. 26 Winter 2002/3.

184. Rudolf Steiner, lecture, Christiania (Oslo) 14 June 1910 and appendix, GA 121, in *The Mission of the Individual Folk Souls*, London: RSP 1970.

185. Sergei O. Prokofieff, *The Vidar Mystery*, Chapter XII in *The Cycle of the Year as a Path of Initiation*, London: TL 1991.

186. Rudolf Steiner, lecture, Bochum 21 December 1913, GA 150, 'The Winter of the Earth and the Spiritual Victory of the Sun', Typescript NSL 171.

187. Rudolf Steiner, lecture, Christiania (Oslo) 21 May 1923, GA 226, in *Man's Being, His Destiny and World Evolution*, Spring Valley: AP, n.b. this quotation appears only in the 3rd edition 1984.

188. Rudolf Steiner, lecture, Christiania (Oslo), 17 June 1910, GA 121, *The Mission of the Individual Folk Souls*.

189. Ibid.

190. 'The Lay of Grimnir', v. 17, in *The Poetic Edda* (see note 182).

191. Manchester: Richard Gill 1892.

192. Keith Ruffles, 'The Kaali Meteor Crater, Saaremaa Island, Estonia', in *The Fortean Times*, FT 297 February 2013.

193. Rudolf Steiner, lecture, Dornach 9 November 1914, GA 158, 'The Connection of Man with the Elemental World. Finland and the Kalevala', Typescript Z 144.

194. Rudolf Steiner, lecture, Helsinki 9 April 1912, GA 136, 'The Essence of National Epics', Appendix II in *Spiritual Beings in the Heavenly Bodies and in the Kingdoms of Nature*, Hudson: AP 1992.

Bibliography

Beowulf, text and translation by John Porter, Hockwold cum Wilton: Anglo-Saxon Books 1995.

Harald Sommerfeldt Boehlke, *The Viking Serpent*, Victoria BC: Trafford Publishing 2007.

Jocelyn Godwin, *Arktos. The Polar Myth in Science, Symbolism and Nazi Survival*, London: Thames and Hudson 1993.

Nicholas Goodrich-Clark, *The Occult Roots of Nazism*, Aquarian Press 1985.

Le Grand Saint Graal or the History of the Holy Grail, translated by Henry Lonelich, AD 1450, from the French Prose 1150–1200 of Sires Robiers de Borron; ed. F.J. Furnivall, Early English Text Society 1874.

Simon James, *The Atlantic Celts. Ancient People or Modern Invention?* London: British Museum Press 1999.

Dan Lindholm, *Stave Churches in Norway*, London: RSP 1969.

Hans Mändl, *Vom Geist des Nordens*, Stuttgart: Mellinger Verlag 1966.

Hamish Miller and Paul Broadhurst, *The Sun and the Serpent*, Launceston: Pendragon Press 1989.

The Poetic Edda, translated by Lee M. Hollander, Austin: University of Texas Press 1990.

The Poetic Edda, translated by Carolyne Larrington, Oxford University Press 1996.

Sergei O. Prokofieff, *The Spiritual Origins of Eastern Europe and the Future Mysteries of the Holy Grail*, London: TL 1993.

Tamara Talbot Rice, *The Scythians*, London: Thames and Hudson 1961.

Joachim Schultz, *Movement and Rhythms of the Stars*, Edinburgh: Floris Books 1986.

Richard Seddon, *Mani. His Life and Work Transforming Evil*. London: TL 1998

Andrew Sinclair, *The Sword and the Grail*, London: Century 1993.

Sone de Nansai, ed. M. Goldschmidt, Tübingen 1899.

Jürgen Spanuth, *Atlantis of the North*, London: Sidgwick and Jackson 1976.

Vilhjalmur Stefansson, *Ultima Thule. Further Mysteries of the Arctic*, London: Harrap 1942.

Rudolf Steiner, *Art as Seen in the Light of Mystery Wisdom*, Dornach 28 December1914–4 January 1915, GA 275, translated by Pauline Wehrle, London: RSP 1996.

—*Christ and the Spiritual World*, Leipzig 28 December 1913–2 January 1914, GA 149, London: RSP 1963.

—'The Etherisation of the Blood', Basel 1 October 1911, in *Esoteric Christianity* GA 130, London: Rudolf Steiner Press 2000.

—*From Symptom to Reality in Modern History*, Dornach 18 October–3 November 1918, GA 185, London: RSP 1976.

—*The Gospel of St Luke/According to Luke,* Basel 15–26 September 1909, GA 114, London: RSP 1988/Great Barrington MA: AP 2001.

—'Greek and Germanic Mythology', Berlin 21 October 1904, GA 92, Typescript Z 331.

—*Karmic Relationships* Vol. VIII, Torquay and London 12–27 August 1924, GA 240, London: RSP 1975.

—*Macrocosm and Microcosm*, Vienna 21–31 March 1910, GA 119, London: RSP 1968.

—'Man in the Earth in Northern and Southern Regions', Dornach 13 October 1923, GA 351, Typescript Z300.

—*Man in the Past, the Present and the Future*, Stuttgart 14–16 September 1923, Dornach 10 September 1923.

—*The Mission of the Individual Folk Souls in Relation to Teutonic Mythology*, Christiania (Oslo) 7–17 June 1910, GA 121, London: RSP 1970

—'The Mystery of the Double. Geographic Medicine', St Gallen 16 November 1917, GA 178, in *Secret Brotherhoods*, Forest Row: RSP 2004

—*Occult Signs and Symbols*, Stuttgart 13–16 September 1907, GA 101, New York: AP 1972.

—'Oral Description of the 1923 Visit to Britain', Dornach 9 September 1923 (GA unknown), see *Rudolf Steiner Speaks to the British*, London: RSP 1998.

—'The Siegfried Saga', Berlin 21 October 1904, GA 92, Typescript Z 331.

—*Spiritual Beings in the Heavenly Bodies and in the Kingdoms of Nature*, Helsinki 3–14 April 1912, GA 136, Hudson: AP 1992.

—*The Sun-Initiation of the Druid Priest*, GA 228, London: RSP 1982.

—*The Temple Legend and the Golden Legend*, 20 lectures, 1904–06, GA 93, London: RSP 1997.

—*True and False Paths in Spiritual Investigation*, Torquay 11–22 August 1924, GA 243, London: RSP 1969.

—*Universe, Earth and Man*, Stuttgart 4–16 August 1908, GA 105, London: RSP 1968.

—*Youth's Search in Nature*, Koberwitz 17 June 1924, GA 217a, Spring Valley: Mercury Press 1979.

Jakob Streit, *Sun and Cross*, Chapter 6, Edinburgh: Floris Books 2004.

Ortrud Stumpfe, *Absturz in den Selbstverrat*, Stuttgart: Mellinger Verlag 1993.

Snorri Sturluson, *Edda*, translated by Anthony Faulkes, London: Dent 1987.

Snorri Sturluson, *Heimskringla (The Norse Kings Sagas)*, Part One, 'The Olaf Sagas', London: J.M. Dent 1970.

Snorri Sturluson, 'The Ynglinga Saga' in *Heimskringla*, London: J.M. Dent 1930.

Tacitus, *Germania (Agricola and Germania)*, London: Penguin Books 2010.

Ernst Uehli, *Nordisch-Germanische Mythologie*, Stuttgart: Mellinger Verlag 1984.

George Vernadsky, *The Origins of Russia. The Ancient Slavs and the World of the Steppes.* Oxford: Clarendon Press 1959.

The Vinland Sagas. The Norse Discovery of America, London: Penguin Books 1965.

Dudley Wright, *Druidism, the Ancient Faith of Britain*, London: Ed. J. Burrow & Co.Ltd. 1924.